I0559577

THROUGH SEA GLASS DARKLY

Second Edition

**A biography
by Clifford Schrage
with afterward
by Sherry Schrage**

Wood Islands Prints,
Prince Edward Island, Canada

ISBN 978-1-987852-36-3

Published by: Wood Islands Prints; 670 TCH Route 1;
Wood Islands, PE C0A 1R0; Canada

The author can be reached via e-mail at
sherryandcliff@gmail.com
web page:
www.cliffschrage.com

Cliff Schrage is a retired high school English teacher
and chaplain. He is a father of eight (six adopted) and grandfather of five. He makes his home with his wife Sherry in
Southeastern Connecticut.

His other books include:
 Silas Dillon of Cary County
A Fruitful Field
Broken Prose, Spoken Poems

DEDICATION

**To our children's children:
Kalaeb, Mercy, Clare, Emma, Finn,
and those that will follow.**

For now
we see through
a glass darkly....

1 Corinthians 13:12

PROLOGUE

They sit at the long table that Saturday morning. She faces the French doors where sunlight falls in the yard—jumbled shade scribbling the lawn. Indian summer opens screens breathing cheeping crickets and October yellow. Husband and wife—eyeglasses on the slopes of noses—laptop before him; jars of sea glass, glue, frames, tools before her   they're together. It's 2019.

"I'm trying to find the right triangle. I need a sail. I got the water and grass." She points.

He looks. "Nice. All those green pieces for grass, like a puzzle. They fit. Blue water too."

"You make them fit. It's easy." She grabs a handful of white pieces—a crackling sound—placing them on the table. Her index finger searches, poking, sliding.

"Enough there to pick from. Get a thin brown piece."

She looks at him doubtfully over the rim of her glasses.

"For the hull, you know, under the sail—the float part of the boat."

"Maybe."

Over the crickets the sound of crows, a neighborhood chainsaw's drone, distant whistle from the Long Island railroad.

"Three weeks. Can't believe it," he says.

"I know."

"Another baby chick flying away."

"You're gonna make me cry."

"I know. Me too."

They're quiet for seconds.

"Seems like yesterday my little girl following me around the yard out there."

Thoughts of wedding day tasks swarm.

"Abby's getting married. Can't believe it. Half of them married now."

Her mind thinks out loud, as though not speaking to him.

"I can't believe it either."

"What are you doing today?"

"Nothing."

Silence.

"Isn't that what you did last Saturday?"

"Yup, not finished doing it."

She giggles.

"Mark Twain said, 'Never put off 'til tomorrow what can be done the day after tomorrow just as well.'"

"Funny."

"Got to stack that wood. Then a doctor appointment—renew my prescription."

"I have an eye doctor appointment at two."

"For?"

"Don't you remember? Have to get this cyst taken off my eyelid."

"Can't even notice it."

"But I do, and it messes my vision a little—annoying. She'll check the pressure in my eyes too—make sure my pressure's not getting worse."

"Shouldn't a skin guy do that? Isn't that dermatology? Removing that?"

"Not this close to the eye. You remind me. I have to make an appointment with the dermatologist. This thing won't heal on my wrist. May be carcinoma again." She sighs.

"'Birthdays of the old require many candles.'"

"I don't get it."

"Candle-lights—doctors, glasses, hearing aids, canes, wheelchairs—all that—candles."

"Stop."

"William Stafford said that."

"We're not old."

"I am. Sixty-two is old."

"I'm only sixty-one."

"For another month." He smiles, eyes peer over glasses at her. "Always said I'd never make sixty. Here we are. Never know when it all ends. Never know who's needed above. Guess they don't need us there." He types.

Silence.

"Sad."

"What?"

"One of us has to go first."

"Maybe not," she said. "Maybe we'll go together." She sips. "Still needed I guess, even though they're grown. Like to think Mercy, Clare, and Emma need us."

"They like us. Wish they didn't live so far." He looks at the yard. "Not fair. Grandkids supposed to be near."

"Who says?"

"I say."

"I wish," she says, placing a slice of glass on a dab of glue.

"Maybe other people need us. Students—who knows." He pokes his finger on some keys. "I'm searching Twain quotes. Start class with a clever quote. Ice breaker gets them thinking. Here's a good one. Want to hear it?"

"Let's hear."

"'I never let my school interfere with my education.'

That's funny."

"Probably true."

"But it works against my job security. Hey this is good: 'Twenty years from now you'll be more disappointed by the things you didn't do than did do.'"

"I would tend to agree."

"Did we do enough?"

"What's enough?"

"I don't know." Some sounds of the crows and the chain-saw in the distance pause their talk again.

"What about this one: 'I've had a lot of worries in my life, most of which never happened.'"

"Definitely true—especially for you."

He smiles.

"You waste all your time not sleeping."

"You're right."

"Mark Twain's right."

She slides pieces of white glass aside, focusing, searching. He scrolls, reading, searching.

"Another good one: 'Man was made at the end of the week when God was tired.'"

"That's silly. He doesn't get tired. Mark Twain has his eye on people. He should be looking at God."

"It's supposed to be humor. He's cynical—about people. That's just it."

"Here's a good piece." She holds it up.

"Let's see." He looks. "Perfect—triangle on an angle, like wind's blowing the sail. Very creative Sherry dear."

"Oh I am not."

"Yes you are. Here's a real Twain-ism: 'I go to heaven for the climate. I go to hell for the company.'"

"Well that's not good. Doesn't work that way."

He laughs. "Of course. He showed his distaste for the hypocrites of his day—probably like any day. Like these days.

His way of mocking the phonies in pulpits and churches."

"But hypocrites don't go to heaven."

"You know that. He probably did too. Just his way of saying."

The old dog Kodi comes and sits beside them. "He's hungry."

"Hello Kodi. There's food in his bowl. He wants to be by us." Cliff pets him, bringing his face close to the dog's, returns to his screen. "Here's a good line: 'Love is when two people know everything about each other and are still friends.'"

She stops a moment, the glue bottle in her hand. "So true." She stares. "'Patient, kind… bears all things… endures all things.' True. Choice—we make—good and bad days. Love is unconditional. I like that."

"Yup. Love is forgiving. A Twain way of saying it."

She looks at her husband—a gentle bearing. He reaches for her hand. "We're still friends," she says.

The two of them with their chins on their chests peer over eyeglasses into one another's eyes. "Hard to believe—living here thirty-eight years this month. Time flies." His thumb pats the back of her hand. "We'll be married forty years soon."

That morning her heart seems to thaw in a dash of fire. "We're still friends," she says again, with a sudden tear. He stands, above, leaning, putting a hand on her shoulder, pressing his face against hers, kissing her cheek, whispering into her ear what the both of them said to one another thousands of times, in myriads of places and circumstances, in hosts of tones, through the last forty-six years together, "I love you."

"Love you too."

PURITY AND PROVISION

1962, Fire Island Pines, New York: the Sayville ferry ride, crammed wagons roll—cla-clump, cla-clump... over curves of boardwalk—down, rising, down again... through shady passageways, sunken forests, grassy dunes, bayberry, beach plum, linseed oil smells blending perfumes of floras and salt air. Cattails, poison ivy, blue view of Great South Bay across to Long Island, faint roar of the Atlantic—it's a long flip-flop hike to the rented beach house.

The sun's touch collides with the ocean's cold. This shocks her feet. "Aahhh!" she squeals thrilled as foamy surf chases her. Backward, forward... running, skipping... shrieking laughs... dueling with the tempo of the rhythm of breakers, until she stands still, staring at the under-tow's white froth sinking her heels—lower, lower with each pass of a wave—down in saturated sand. She marvels with four-year old wonder.

What could a pint-size girl know about a God larger than the universe? Excited, curious, squinting in blue light, Sherry plays creatively in pearly sand—pails, shovels, sieves, sand clinging like sugar on slight calves and arms. With the Atlantic's cadent waves thumping, climbing the ascent of shore, she hears pipes of plovers, yells of gulls, the breathing of waves.

What could her perception be of the unseen all-seeing eye watching her steps, thoughts, dreams, play? Who has the numbers of hairs on her head and days of her life? What thoughts of His wisdom, omnipresence, power? What could be the scope of her grasp of a predetermined reliability to lead her one day into His ways? Sea-green irises set in an unsullied face look with trust and natural longing for love—since age two reaching always with arms—to be held and hugged, to dance with Pop-Pop, with Daddy, with Uncle Bob.

Tall hoary dunes shaped like waves, erupting white and barrier-like, bulky—in grazed strokes of beach grass, oppose the ocean surf.

She's engrossed in a meticulous world of castle building, singing quietly, dissuading her three-year-old brother away from what she's building. "Mommy! Gary kicked my sand castle! Tell him to stop!" Squinting eyes plead for justice.

What kind of awareness of God's single-minded attention on every minuscule detail of a tiny girl, of a lost earth? She's four, intent on her own little creation, barely aware of the human duties—to provide for her. Those jobs are Daddy's. "Always sweating!" He works in the greenhouse "all the time!" He sends his family on summer vacations, this thirty-two-mile sliver of silver sand, once in the far past a mere sand bar, now a white-green barricade fronting the striking Atlantic, shielding Long Island's south shore. Long Island itself, with its abutting islands, spans more than a hundred miles, extends like a larger sliver, a fish-shaped sandbar that has lain over the centuries—its glacier scars on the north shore.

"I wish Daddy could be here!"

"Me too," says Gary.

Thoughts, scoops of sand, a song springs from her voice—improvised—of Daddy. Fine tufts of blonde locks waft before her eyes. Avoiding wet sandy fingers she uses a wrist, brushing them from her vision. She's unaware, can't distinguish these days as some of the happiest—now, but she's conscious of how much she loves the beach, long happy days, ice cream cones, waking mornings here… "I love the beach!" she says.

Gary stumbles onto her castle, collapsing the bucket-shaped forms of sand. "Ohhhh!" she cries, protests. "Mommy he wrecked it!" Tears. He stands, looking. Sherry waits, looking at the damage, at Mommy. "He always does that!"

"He didn't mean to."

"I'm finding things!" she says, dropping her shovel, stepping closer to the sea with her bucket. Down in her growing intelligence she learns from Mommy that she needs to fight anger, to be poised with Gary, to be a big sister. "He can have my castle!" She steps away.

Down by the surf—it's the trifling things she wants—shells, smooth stones, slivers of driftwood, crab claws, surprises. She postures them in her bucket, first perusing, prizing. She wipes sandy fingers across her shirt, her favorite flowery one—"the one for the beach" with the neat little row of pockets at the lower extremity. Little fingers push aside strands of hair from eyes. Warmth of sand on her feet gives her a perceptible feeling of safety—her whole self—a curious comfort.

This is another creative adventure—her assorted collection, "finding things." In her little world she leans, seizes, stares at whitened glass flat in her opened palm, the size of two fingers. She's absorbed with its semi-transparency. Sea glass—old, ocean worn, storm beaten glass. To her they're nicer, lighter stones, favored finds—unaware they were sharp broken shards earlier decades—clear glass transfigured to pearl white—like Fire Island itself.

Beach walkers pass, "Adorable," a voice above her. What's adorable? she wonders. Me? My things?

Adorable—a four-year-old. Durable—that's glass—the broken shattered creations, sturdy-smooth, distinctive pieces on the shore in the surf—proven, resilient, enduring in singular finalized brokenness. It's a paradox—durable in brokenness. This little find, this piece once a shining translucence, glass made white through time—a fragment purified—spotless white, she holds in her unblemished palm, a pure pearl-lustered keepsake.

She places it in her bucket, looks at it among the array inside.

She feels good about this one. Her small heart smiles. "Mommy!" she shouts above a thump of a wave, stepping higher up to Nancy reading her magazine. "Look! This rock. I found it!" She holds it up, smiling.

"Oooo," said Nancy. "That's sea glass. Very nice."

Gary comes close, peering from Sherry's shoulder, looking.

Sherry puts it before her little brother. He touches. "Oooo," he says. "See nice glass."

"Sea glass?" her wondering eyes—intent.

"Old piece of broken glass. Waves made it pretty," Nancy adds from behind her magazine. "Years and years."

Sherry peruses, thinking. "Beach glass!" Nancy adds.

"Beach glass?" Her knees bend. A little dance, a foot kicks in impulse of happiness. She twirls, back toward the shore, eager for more. She stops, pulls the glass from the bucket of shells, places it like a prize into one of her shirt's pink patterned pockets. By the day's end these pockets and bucket will be filled with favored finds. She is unaware, but does inherently feel sheltered, secure, mysteriously safe in unseen hands.

***

TEREBELLUM SHELL

A conch,
A little augur,
Shiny-slim,
Glossy-smooth,
Pacific shell
Sand dweller
In bullet shape
With short spire
In soft pastel
Wan patterns of
Sand colors, in shape

Like the pattern on
This thin page,
A sub-tidal find,
Finished in time,
A piece of pretty
 Death to cherish
And carry away
For keeps.

Once after a childish clash with Mom and two-year-old Gary, "I'm leaving!" she says, arms folded.

"Oh really. Will you pack a bag?"

"Yes. I'm packing a bag!" An angry righteous frown.

She packs a paper bag—toys, stuffed animals, but can't open the door herself. Mom opens, she marches out. The door closes behind her. She's had enough of rules, deciding to go on her own. She sits on the porch. In an hour she realizes she's thirsty. She knocks on the door. The door soon opens.

Brief, daring, yet it's a clear expression of rebellion.

In later years she'll realize—that if that runaway were interrupted—Mom stopping her exit—she may have resisted: "I don't need you. I'm smarter than the rules here," deepening her small willfulness. She eventually learns that Mommy's love isn't short lived. There is this phenomenon called love—always unconditional. She could rely on a higher parent-power that comes to her aid, no matter, to promptly open the door, no matter how faint her knock.

Pop-pop, Daddy's dad, adoringly teases his grand-daughter—always to kindle adorable reactions. "And who do you think you are anyhow?" he says, bending low smiling at her absorbing eyes.

"I'm not anyhow. I'm Sherry!"

"Oh who do you think you are anyhow Sherry?" "I'm Sherry! Who's 'anyhow?'"

He laughs with his singular loud laugh. Her grin materializes like sunshine. "Who's anyhow?"

In 1963 Pat Pisani has to work again as the family budget can't afford him the vacation. He sends them.

But this year Gary is sick, forced under a tent by the boardwalk. Chicken pox—its misery passes through his slight frame. As much as her brother could be a pest, these two are loyal buddies. At five she pities him. He can't play by the shore. Tent shade and discomfort imprison him. She stays near, includes him, shows him things.

Boyish mischief moves Gary in his childhood. The greenhouse where Daddy and Pop-Pop work across the street is a world of green soil, noise, fixtures, cuttings, machinery, oil, water—a hot wet humidor-like place drenched with fascinations for curious boys who admire working men. Four-year old Gary's freedom leads him to a watering machine, propelled with gas power, pullies, rumbling roars, a rapid spinning belt with twists and turns. His small hand holds a stick, poking, jabbing, daring it near its rugged loudness, its rough grown man madness, sending it into the raucous spin. It pulls. His small hand refuses release, not promptly realizing danger. His hand yanks into the mechanism, suddenly severing four fingers—as swiftly as the belt spins.

Sherry arrives from kindergarten to a vacant house greeted by bloody clothes, red blots strewn on the floor and stairway. She feels an unfamiliar aura drawn from the loudness of that bloody silence. "Mommy? Mommy!" Terror pushes her to sobbing.

A long time. Finally Nanny races in, the rest of the family's at Brookhaven Hospital.

Three of Gary's four severed fingers are salvaged, re—attached. A long month of the white bandage mitten is embedded into their young remembrances. Early in their lives they find in the details of that distressful loss a new awareness of human vulnerability. Years of play swirl quietly in their memory beneath the traumatic, the unusual. Memories built around images of shock seem to remain the clearest in young minds.

In 1964 Pat devotes evenings to painting the house. Scaffolds, ladders, paint cans, drop cloths, white trim, blue siding—all this chimes appealingly through Gary's and Sherry's senses. They watch excited about the new color, the active bustle. In August the job is done. One weekday the town trucks arrive to tar the road for the bluestone foundation. Sherry and Gary decide to "help Daddy." They get sticks, dipping into the hot tar, scuttling back and forth from the road to the side of the house, daubing tar onto the newly painted siding, simulating Daddy's efforts, "helping Daddy." Mommy's inside unsuspecting—in the days when kids were sent outdoors in mornings to play, unrestrained, eating their lunch delivered onto the stoop, coming in safely in the evening.

Nanny visits while Daddy's at work. "Oh my God!" Knowing her son's temperament, she discards the sticks, rushes these two into her car before Pat returns from work to this black mess on the painted siding, their clothes and skin, hurrying them to her home to clean them and protect them from Daddy's anger.

Suspense fades with time until Sherry and Gary, hidden in Nanny's screened room, hear the slammed door of Daddy's car. At five and six they listen to the voices at the front door. "Where are they?" His shouts are frightening. "They ruined the whole side of the house!"

"They thought they were helping you. They're staying here. Go home. Cool down Pat. I'm not letting you near them. No! No! They're hidden. You can't find them." This duel at the front door of Nanny's house, from behind the closed screen room freezes them with confusion. "Nanny guards us," Gary murmurs.

On another hot day that summer the two of them decide they need a pool in their yard. They pull spade shovels from the hooks in the garage and dig—for hours—on the lawn beside the swing-set. Somehow they manage an oval shaped eight foot wide hole—clods of grass piled beside a foot "deep enough to swim," then injecting the hose, aiming to fill, wondering why it wouldn't. But the mud and the running water was cool anyway—hose water gushing for hours.

"What are you two doing?" Mom shouts out the window. "Making a pool!" Gary shouts with confidence.

"Daddy's not gonna be happy."

Queen Anne's lace, daisies, dandelions, chicory, black eyed Susans—Sherry pulls them from the field beside the Lakeland Avenue greenhouses where traffic flows south from Sunrise Highway. Throngs of customers from the city—Fire Island bound—enter Pop-Pop's business. Six-year old Sherry sets up her own "shop" outside the door. Rubber bands hold wildflower bouquets upright in a vase on a nylon chair.

"Adorable!"

She's heard that before.

"And how much is a bouquet of your lovely flowers?" "Quarter." Sherry looks up, squinting.

Gary sits beside her at his table. Lemonade pitcher, cups, 10 cents. "May I have a cup of your lemonade please?"

He struggles as he pours, spilling. A floating bug swims inside the nice lady's cupful. "Oh there's a bug," he says. "Don't worry. I get him." He pokes soiled fingers, finding the creature, pinning it to the side of the cup, sliding it up, out, flicking it with spraying fingers, wiping his pants. "There," he says.

"Oh thank you very much," the lady's smiles simulate sips.

Uncle Bob's the fun adult. There were episodes of "sledding," seated on the card table flipped upside-down, tugging them on hills behind the greenhouse. Visits to the zoo, New York City, the racetrack, the diner… are planted Uncle Bob memories.

This is the year the two of them look forward to drives in the back of the gas-fumed 49' Plymouth, seated unrestrained on milk crates, falling forward when Daddy brakes, backward giggling accelerating forward.

Days playing on Grove Street include bolting sprints to the back of the house when the gravel truck roars down the normal quietness. In excited thrill they pretend, "The monster!" shrieking, holding their ears, ducking beneath weeping willow limbs, shutting their eyes.

Sherry turns seven, and Robbie's born in January 1965. This new member brings an adventure. She's permitted to help.

He's a live doll, but she gains a mature profundity—trusted with small measures of regular care—her first practice with an infant. She likes this. Nancy's teaching gives confidence. She sings to him, makes him giggle, holds his bottle, burps, comforts him with grown-up simulation in his fussing.

Daddy's parents Pop-Pop and Nanny own the greenhouses where Daddy works. One 1966 afternoon seven-year-old Gary takes his new BB gun to the field, sits atop a mulch pile hill, and finds targets to shoot: the windows on the greenhouse. He sits fixedly, "innocently" pumping his gun, aiming, shooting, hearing amusing clatter of glass. Again he surprises the world with mischief. Pop discovers what's happening. From inside the glass exterior, gradually unmuffled by Gary's razing of the transparent walls, the sound of his cursing—Italian hollers—becomes a strident shrill.

Sherry hears as Gary gets his howling spanking. Daddy has to replace every pane. "Why did you do this?"

"I wanted to try my gun you got me."

There's something pivotal in the love of grandparents. While parenting is hard, grand parenting is bracing restorative, the bliss that colors the black and white of senior living. Grand parenting bears love's velvety expression, often the forbearance of God; while parenting calls for stouter expressions—both speckled with human error.

Nanny's doting indulgence gushes from the gap of a missing daughter she had wished for. She gives and gives, making a lot of sound about it. Naturally Sherry welcomes it, exploits it. The earliest image in her recall is once seated in a highchair at Nanny's house on Manton Street with an adoring Nanny offering more attention than busy Nancy could in a week. That obsessive love is the reminiscence flashing as the earliest star in the sky of Sherry's memory. It's that attention that makes it feasible for even a one-year old to retrieve long afterward.

Memories of Daddy are muddled. His first purpose is provision—not failing bringing home bread—utensils to eat it with, the table to eat at… Before becoming a county sheriff, that providing demands sixty work hours weekly.

There's something crucially honorable about any man who sacrifices for his family.

Provision and Purity merge, convening like water and air in youthful life. "Let the little children come to Me …. for of such is the Kingdom of God." Purity displays her emblem through translucence of clear glass. It lights in clarity, finishes in whiteness. *"Before the throne there was a sea of glass, like crystal."* (Revelation 4:6) *"And the street of the city was pure gold, like transparent glass."* (Revelation 21:21)

Little girls wear angelic faces. Slices of sea glass endure as tokens of hope—give backs—refined, weathered, shattered fragments of man's manufacturing, labors at creation—as God creates. Man, manufactured in the image of God, clothed with God's orientation to create, deploys himself to accomplish just that—to create, finish. Glass, clear and whole, broken—initially trash—someway given to the heaving of the sea—worn, fallen, smooth; broken and lost like man—transformed from purity of transparency to purity of whiteness—is reclaimed to the treasure hold of a child.

The shade of white in the daisy, the color of fallen snow, the manner of the bride, the hue of albumen in the egg—tints of innocence and purity—the white cap in the wave—its closing foaming finish on the shore—that whiteness occasions the resulting color of fragments of translucent glass in a broken world, finally wearing opacity, finding its way into the pocket of a cherisher.

Referring to a tuft of flowers passed by eyes from a speeding train, Robert Frost said, *"Heaven gives its glimpses only to those not in position to look too close."* Maybe. Or maybe hints of heaven are given in lasting reflections everywhere: the child's smile, discoveries by the sea, the ice cream cone, the vacation, the kind hand of a grandmother, the newborn, the white mitten bandage, the assiduous father, new glass in the window, the open door, the welcome home, the willow, a childhood ride on a makeshift sled…

Sea glass lain in the debris of death of shellfish skeletons, retrieved from the turmoil of time's storms on the world's shores, prized in the palm of the finder; like men, glass shaped and shaded opaque, beautiful in brokenness, lovely as stones, purified by tempests, frail simplicities—all distinct, all devised by a detail-conscious creator, are fallen yet chosen, broken yet prized, sought for, found, kept, cherished.

A TIME TO THROW AWAY
Search memory,
Rummage under rubble
In moth-balled cellar
Or yellowed past.
Dig out debris, dross,
Worthless odds, ends
Fit for the trash heap.
Toss them there to fester
In fires of burning forgetfulness
Forever.

Search memory,
Carefully slide out,
Wash, polish, shine
Those items of returned desire.

Find the worthwhile pieces
For the window show—out, festive—
Show to those who remember tomorrow
The final fires of His refining
The crucible for silver.

VERDURE

The middle school years—that unripe vernal season, arrive, deafening Sherry's ability to hear, "You're beautiful," though those words may have been spoken. She doesn't learn her worth, no longer hears the word "adorable." Pure jade—a gem among many dark green stones, she's an emerald island, a shy, self-conscious green. Feeling lost in the customary greenness of life's commonplaceness, she searches in crowded mazes of middle school life, searching out her own exquisite green somewhere in the enormously glorious veronica-green of the world.

Green irises—two islands among two ponds of white—green vestibules surrounding deep pupil-windows opening to a quiet, inner self; windows before blue-yellow, are youthful eyes, are docile irises born in the greenhouse, born behind sheltering glass made green by life within, rising inside.

GREENHOUSES
Emerald buildings,
Transparent iridescence,
Shells in symmetry—
God's vision through and
Into thin human skins,
Symmetrical order—immortal
Life residing within.
Limpid transparency
Pulsating greenness
Of life rising from wet, hot loam
All glowing through.

Middle school holds a crest of the unseasoned, the verdant stage in the life cycle: the green, immature, unripe, wan, untrained, naïve, gullible, vulnerable, the unready. Sherry is in the greenroom, that sitting room in the theater where performers wait before the entrance onto the stage. It's the waiting room of the world, and as Shakespeare sees it, "All the world's a stage."

God is the author of color, as man may mean for it to mean more than pure adornment. The greenhorn is the inexperienced, untutored human moving through youth somewhere between childhood and adulthood. It's that phase when all seems to explode in disharmony: legs, then torso; emotions, then reason—that part when everything sprouts unsynchronized, between the bud and the ripening.

A violent voice speaks, "You're ugly and unlovable." It's not a human voice. And no affable voice tells her, "You're pretty.

You're valuable." At least she doesn't hear one. She is lost in all the green, a jungle in a giant greenhouse of a world, finding her way. She's a wallflower, the flora in the corner of the wide field: unobtrusive, scared, quiet, hiding in hiding places, unsure of her distinct greenness fitting anywhere.

"Ugly," she says to the mirror with tears. Awkward is what she feels. Neither athletic, musical, artistic, social, nor especially brilliant, her unobtrusive hiding in frail quietness becomes the bull's eye on her back.

Shakespeare chooses green in *Othello* as the color for jealousy's eyes, and he picks the generic monster to personify it. What grows in Sherry's vista is a scrutiny of jealousy, a desire to be this other girl—one ostensibly confident; one seemingly sure of herself; one forward, boisterous, unintimidated; one school boys chase. The paradox is fixed: some of the girls envy her—her prettiness, her virtue. Mean girls perch at their meanest height at the school yard.

It's 1968, grade six. For some unknown reason one loud

bully persuades—as a tyrant does toadies, subjects who fear her—nearly all the girls in class—to shun Sherry, ignore her completely, and let her know she's shunned. This gang-up on one—a "bruised reed," persists for weeks.

"What's wrong with me? All my friends are gone." She can't sleep, and is too ashamed to mention to any, especially Mom. Irrational dread follows: if I'm rejected at school, I'll be rejected at home. She imagines. I can't tell Mom; she'll be ashamed of me. Shame seems to salivate at the heels of rejection like a hungry dorsal finned devourer, following the crashing wake of rejection, sealing a person into silence.

Early winter, the bell ends a dark school day during the solstice. A sheet of slushy snow on the ground, long tree shadows like woeful fingers stretching. Suddenly strangely the girls in class befriend her again. Pats on the back. "Let us walk you home! Sherry we want to be friends now!"

"Why?"

"Because we like you."

"But why did you ignore me?"

"We didn't ignore you."

"But you did. Everybody did. What did I do wrong?"

"We like you now."

The busy commotion of a school day's end lulls in pause of the day's transition: kids walking, boarding buses.

Why this sudden friendly welcoming into the sixth-grade girls' social circle again? It's as mysterious as was the sudden arbitrary rejection, as mysterious as the "mystery of iniquity" that could even reside in an eleven-year old bully's heart. In the bleakest season of the year the cold strangeness of this keeps Sherry from conceding into the apparent warmth of kindliness. They all exit the gate of the school yard, a flock of bewildering sham friendliness around her. Right outside the school gate on Grove Street, "Now!" the plotter shouts.

Eleven girls each slip out a prepared arsenal of frozen snowballs—ice balls—encircling as wolves, swarming as bees, and all begin at close range propelling, hurling, cackling, laughing.

One stony ball smashes the side of her head, deafening; one to the chin draws blood from lips; a third bangs bluntly to the face, drawing blood from her nose. Flashes of white darts miss. The suddenness of such meanness stuns. The lengthy betrayal is amplified by this duplicity, this bizarre plotted design.

Rejection—real or imagined—is loud, violent—a precursor to a loneliness of the most agonizingly raw, throbbing, deafening kind. Its cold rends a heart, bringing shame to the rejected, then confines in cold interment—covered for dignity, for fear of further rejection. It imprisons into isolation. Rejection is a sadistic numbing ice ball to the heart—especially an eleven year—old girl's. It is the swollen face of betrayal. Its violence arrives in numerous faces to all the world—the divorce, the abandonment, the estrangement....

Outside, nine-year old Gary runs with brave resistance to his sister's rescue, hurling, throwing snow in defense, punching girls, frantically scattering the swarm, shouting, alleviating the attack, screaming threats, enraged, making way for his sister to get to the front door. She enters, leaking blood, tears, cries.

Mom receives her with confusion, annoyance.

"What happened? What's going on?" She shouts at the street from the door toward girls fused tightly in giggling fear.

Sherry cries, holding her face, her ear.

"It's those girls. They hit Sherry with ice balls!" Gary is shouting. The pack of girls run down the street—cackling hyena—like laughs scuttling with them. Sherry's obliged to her brother Gary, the only warm spot this afternoon.

Nancy's friend Mary is visiting this day—always well dressed, confident, a wealthy woman—Aunt Mary whom Sherry reveres nearly to idolizing. This timing could not be worse. Mortification is what she feels—embarrassment—the glazing finish. Sherry has stepped into a hollow that makes her want to die. What must Aunt Mary think of me? I'm a girl no girls like? Something's wrong with me. What's wrong with me?

School the next day means Mom's escort to the principal's office. Demands are made. There's a one-at-a-time string of mean girls—and of fearful green toadies who obey mean girls. It's a procession into the principal's office—all participants of violence, contributors of the invisibly whispered plot to reject one, accomplices unaware of a world of unseen demons—to disallow one. It becomes a cavalcade of coerced public apologies, some with clandestine grins, some with authentic remorse and faces of shame—like Macbeth's vacant gaze at his hands in disbelief at his deeds, *"What hands are here! Ha, they pluck out mine eyes."* Eleven-year old girls shocked by their own cruelty incited by one makes a school administration see it as a necessary method for mending.

The second half of that school year continues in that pain of shame, confusion, and self-loathing. "What's wrong with me? What's wrong with people?" She feels her loneliness—a tangled knit of awareness of confusion. In later decades she'll understand that this is the human race—has been, for generations, millennia.

Twenty years earlier her mom Nancy suffered the ache of rejection, the consciousness of being discarded, abandoned— mysteriously—by her own father, Sherry's other grandfather—abruptly at eleven. Afterward enrolled in a local Christian school, Nancy was taught the Bible, the assurances of a loving heavenly Father; but later in high school, further in life, she declines any inclusion of faith life, scarcely even mention of a heavenly Father. Rejection through abandonment by a father to a young girl can be wreckage, a hurricane to a sea-level shore, one only God can mend.

Twenty hundred years earlier the rejection of the Messiah was certain—a betrayal forecast at the birth of time, inscribed in foreshadowings in ancient days in the scriptures, *"He is despised and rejected by men, a Man of sorrows and acquainted with grief. And we hid, as it were, our faces from Him; He was despised, and we did not esteem Him."* (Isaiah 53:2) 750 years later the pivotal event was alluded to by Jesus Himself. His betrayer was identified, his end sealed, his mode signaled by a kiss. That rejection, clarified at supper beforehand, unleashed by religious frauds, was bought with silver, applied with foreigners' icy fists, completed on a tree that had once flourished in green, replete with flowing sap, becoming the place His mortal blood spilled. That betrayal, part of the sovereign plan, like all human suffering, a mysterious permission, a nod granted by an all loving monarch, granting life through death, deploying us to continue *"looking unto Jesus, the author and finisher of our faith, who for the joy that was set before Him endured the cross, despising the shame."* (Hebrews 12:2) Final cries from the place of the culmination of rejection: *"My God, My God, why have you forsaken Me?"*

It's in these middle school years her Nanny brings her to worship on Sundays. Sherry savors the mystery found in Sunday worship, reveres the ritual, the loftiness in solemnity, but mostly surveys a faintly curious prospect of somehow actually knowing God personally. She and Nanny are the only family members who practice any faith. Trickles of scripture reading during the mass drip into her ears. She marvels at stories of Jesus' birth, miracles, parables, His death, the resurrection. In this verdant stage she longs for more.

"The Charley Brown Christmas," celebrated Charles Schulz's story about the rejected tree, decorated honorably for Christmas—as memory tells—becomes an early site for Sherry to taste this living water. As the tale closes, Linus recites the ancient passage from Luke's gospel in chapter two: *"Now there were in the same country shepherds living out in the fields, keeping watch over their flock by night..."* the angel, the city of David, the Savior, Christ the Lord, the sign, the Babe wrapped, the multitude of heavenly host, the night sky revealing the visible creation. That abbreviated disclo-

sure of the fulfilling advent of the epochs, like a glass of water enlivening in her young heart, makes her inquisitive; but without sufficient understanding. *"For there is born to you this day in the city of David a Savior, who is Christ the Lord."* Luke 2:11

REJECTION
It shades in hoary grays—
Shadows in ashen gloom, overcast
As in the unreturned, "Hello."

You're unfit for the shelf,
Not worth the work, rework,
Any renovation, reconciliation;

Unfit for the attic,
Amiss, out of tune, missing strings, keys,
You're remiss refuse.

Distressing message
Found in a bottle afloat,
"We're sorry but... we regret to inform you..."

The college, position, proposal
divorce, denial, door slam,
Unanswered mail—

It shades in hoary grays—
Shadows in ashen gloom, overcast:
As in the returned, "I don't want you."

It's in those autumn days when her life first converges with this kid Cliff. At ten, eleven, twelve, he has this crush on this quiet Sherry, this girl with golden hair often visiting her friends in his nearby neighborhood. He drops his baseball glove, soccer ball, convincing Mike, Tom, Gene, Marty, and Rick to play Ringolevio with the girls.

A kind of hide-and-seek game, Ringolevio is played with two teams. One team runs and hides. The other counts to one hundred, then searches for the other team. There's a "jail"—a bench in the middle of the apartment complex. When the searching team captures all the hiding team members, the objective is reached. Any pursuer can catch any on the pursued side by clutching, holding, and chanting "Ringolevio 1-2-3, 1-2-3, 1-2-3!" If the caught one breaks free during the quick recitation, he or she is not caught and is considered still "in." If caught, then he's taken to jail. But any "in" member of the hiding team can liberate jailed team members by barging into the jail without being caught, tagging the captives shouting "Ringolevio free, Ringolevio free...."

Boys consent to games with the girls. Counting, Cliff spies, watching the direction Sherry runs to hide. He "finds" her in bushes, behind a tree, crouching beside a structure. She is pretty, with long flaxen hair, a smile like sunshine. She smells clean, her laughing voice is magical. She doesn't run fast. She's first to be seized—his capture. He holds her, chanting, "Ringolevio one two three, one two three, one two three!" declaring it slowly, holding her sweet life for as long as he can, and then he escorts her to jail. The first prisoner. He volunteers to be the guard, prolonging nearness to this mysterious Sherry.

Teams reverse and Sherry turns to seek, and Cliff is sure to give himself, surrendering his "hiding" place for her to find him. When she seizes him, his sham resistance to break free is unnoticed. These captures are where he finds the girl of his grammar school dreams' enchanting fragrance.

Middle school life passes. Sherry walks to and from school alone, avoiding aggressions on the bus. One day, passing a length of split rail fence on her two-mile trek home, she finds in a notch on the top of a post a shining quarter, half hidden. She slides it out with elation, wondering—who? Why? When? These discoveries are daily, anticipated, an exciting highlight of her walk—sometimes a nickel, sometimes a dime, quarter, once a dollar. Her ingenuous mind surmises it's an old person liberally designing from his or her own loneliness—angelically watching this young girl, suspecting her loneliness, delighting as Sherry hurries to the notch. It remains a mystery, originating from some kind hand, maybe from heaven.

Another enigmatic episode comes once walking home upset about a test—her seventh grade final in math. Trudging in June heat an old woman stops her. "What's wrong young lady? Why are you upset?" She surveys Sherry's face.

"I took my final math test and I think I failed. My worst subject." Tears fall.

"You didn't fail. You passed. Don't worry. Don't be upset."

Somehow she feels relief. "Thank you," she recalls saying.

This voice, this person never seen or heard before or after, and this encounter becomes another memorable mystery.

Test results do turn out fine.

It's another one of those sunny days that stamps an immobile pause in time. 1970, summer preceding eighth-grade, boarding the ferry to Fire Island with friends; midsummer breezes add to the anticipation. They tread across the thin width of Fire Island to spread their blankets. Sherry takes a walk with one friend midday for awhile. The surf's music eases adolescent tensions; her eyes search for the rare piece of glass. The pieces of driftwood—trunks of trees, weathered milled lumber, bleached branches, small roots practically weightless and worn like parts of hands that have lost their grip on the eroding earth—are arrayed with brittle shells of dead crabs, white shells of surf clams, and dried blackened seaweed tassels.

But she's after glass. White slices, and as memory recalls, one big green piece—bleached, round, dulled from its gloss—finds her sight. The smooth satin bottom of a bottle, an addition to home's assortment—bottle-green like her eyes, green as the greenhouses, icon of verdant youth's growth.

It's the transience of green, the ironic, ever impermanence of fading green, green found in broken green bottles, shattered bygone fragments, washed, feathered, time-smoothed, emerald-green holding the reminder of the impermanence of youth; emerald-green reminding of the brevity of youth. This prized iridescence of olive glass caught on the shoreline, removed, made permanent as stone, holds a tinge in perpetuity, freezes time.

It's in these days Grandpa Joe, Nancy's step-dad, dies. Twelve—year-old Sherry stands over his open casket, perusing—her first glowering stare at human death—a loss that rouses her young heart to fearful tears and confused thoughts of that human closure, and that mysterious God, that distant One she at no time airs into plain language, "I want Him," but unmindfully within cries to know.

She reminisces:

"Come on kids we're going to pick mushrooms!" Grandpa shouts with a laugh.

She and Gary carry buckets into the woods with Grandpa Joe to collect mushrooms. He knows which ones are safe. He warns pointing at the poisonous. It's that thrill of simple collecting that makes this exciting. And it's that innate tremor of avoiding the mysterious poisonous evil as well.

Another week, "Tomorrow's Saturday. Will you kids help me pick dandelions?"

With nods of eagerness their undersized, clumsy green selves move closer to him—this man born in Czechoslovakia who makes them feel more treasured than mushrooms or dandelions. He makes wine in the cellar. This is a secrecy, but Grandpa Joe's happiness has a magical way of painting everything. Sherry and Gary are engrossed with his animated colors, expressive tones, laughing finishes.

Another weekend evening, "Let's go catch some crabs!"

Crabbing means big fish heads in galvanized traps, fish tails tied to lines and dock cleats, the rotting tails weighted sunken to the sandy floor, lines taut, minded—gently felt with soft tugs—slipped up slowly when a crab is on. Sherry waits with the net, ready, scooping blue clawed crabs until the bucket is filled with this collection of crawling clawing treasures, late until daylight shrinks.

Now, Grandpa Joe's light has ebbed, and Sherry looks on this display—this death expression in the funeral home—hands folded over his middle, body enclosed in a suit never worn in the woods, fields, or by the bay. It's hard to behold, prodding her into those memories, sobbing a hundred noisy tears. She thinks of how often she sat by this warm man—in the radiance of his talk and smiles.

After his leaving she's shadowed by fears of death. Fears of losses impair her entrance into adolescence. Months of worried imaginings of others' deaths to follow, alarming imaginings of ghostly visitations—Grandpa passing in a car, in the crowded market, his voice in the field, his laughing in her sleep. Grandpa Joe, the nice man who stepped into their lives, marrying Nancy's mom Madeline a decade after Nancy's dad abandoned, making that vacant hole for Joe to fill. He presence was like the bright side of the moon.

Doubt, joy, fear, goodwill, anger, love, jealousy, grief.... the record of human sentiments—some needing resistance, some working through—stretches long; and life to a child can seem ominous and bleak. No such thing as grief counseling those days. No one talks about his leaving, or any hope that grief will diminish, or any hope of any reunion after it all.

On the Sayville acreage an enormous white pine falls in a storm. Bark has pealed in the tree's splitting, baring proof the old tree was still growing, sap-flooded, sap-green, healthy before its plummet. It lived more than eighty years, still suggesting years left to shade the world, if it were not twisted and leveled by a sudden tornado driven gust.

Years pass, and aging works; the outward human declines, but the inner man may develop, growing strong until death.

From youth, even with all life's wounds, how unspoiled it is to grow in grace, to continue growing, contributing to service of others, to grow green and strong like a stately pine, right until we fall, the way Grandpa Joe lived and died.

RECOVERIES & REBOUNDS

Unlike stones, light passes through those pieces whose color bleeds between orange and black—that dull gilt or golden brown found in lusters which decades earlier shone glossy, now shows in low luster—the diaphanous color of ale—softened to copper resplendence blending in with sand and stones on the shoreline.

Set on a shelf—jars of sea glass in browns—a fleck of blends filling the lucidity in a mix of a hundred sundry tints, each piece is distinct in shape and color. What the same sun, salt, pounding does to one piece of glass—changes from piece to piece—as buffetings through years do to human lives. All the fragments of broken lives glow with immortally infinite meaning in the artistic scheme of God's majestic mosaic.

The same strong wind that strengthens the oak, topples the poplar. "I will sing of mercy and judgment." (Psalms 101:1) The fire that comforts can also destroy. "Come, and let us return to the Lord; for He has torn, but He will heal us; He has stricken, but He will bind us up."

Each human bears exactly forty-six chromosomes, and somehow coexists in distinction, all special, not one more special than another. All ordinary, human, similar; yet extraordinary, dissimilar; all with some varying amount of brown dye in the skin's pigment, all in diverse shapes, are all made in God's image, yet each one extraordinary in millions of facets, qualities, idiosyncrasies seen and unseen that have peculiar beauty in themselves.

Sherry proceeds into high school, blossomed visibly into a striking beauty. She's taken on more of her mom's flaxen Northern Europe than Dad's Mediterranean. It doesn't take long for boys' attentions to unveil; they're often upperclassmen. The phone rings. "Hello?" Nancy answers.

"Hi may I speak with Sherry?"

"Who is this?"

"This is Rich," the deep voice murmurs.

"Just a minute." Nancy covers the phone's speaker. "Where's Sherry?"

"Doing homework in her room."

"Sherry!"

"Yeah?"

"Telephone."

She descends, lifts the receiver in the living room. "I got it!" Nancy hangs up in the kitchen. "Hello."

"Hello Sherry, this is Rich."

"Hi?"

"I wonder if you'd go to the movies Friday, with me. Sayville theater?"

"Sure."

"Okay. Great. Get you at seven?"

"That's fine. You know where my house is?"

"Yes I do. Grove Street."

"Okay!"

He doesn't say what's playing.

Those months pass. Another call: "Hello may I speak with Sherry?"

"Who is this?"

"This is Bob."

Calls, knocks, flirtations, invitations... social circles widen. She wins a class officer election in her class of four hundred, finds a place of acceptance without searching, despite the nagging fatiguing self-opinion of rejection, unworthiness, hurt. It's a paradox. Why and how—with an unobtrusive personality—this popularity and recognition? Well, she's pretty.

Old Nanny and Pop-Pop move in at home because of his stroke. Pat has secured a good job as a deputy sheriff with the county. A habit of gambling has intruded into the house.

Retirement with Pop and Nanny's windfall from selling the greenhouses opens excess time inviting Friday night poker games, trips to the Racetrack, and daily drives to the bookie.

On a visit to the track one summer night, Pop-Pop with his regular five gambling buddies buy their bets, sit down to wait for the races to begin. They talk horses, cards, money. One of them, Bing, is uncommonly quiet, until "What's it feel like when you have a stroke Pat?"

"Everything gets fuzzy like." A silent still stare.

"Hey. Bing. You awright? Bing?"

"Sumpins wrong wit Bing," Eddie says.

"He's just starin. What's wrong wit Bing?"

Bing's eyes are a vacant stare. He's still.

"Bing's dead. Fellas, Bing's dead. Look, he's stone dead." The old men look at their old friend seated there with betting stubs on his lap."

"What should we do? The race is startin," Watson says.

"I gotta go place a bet. Wait. I gotta get to the window before the next race," Eddie says.

Silence. These eighty-year-olds look at each other. There's shock, but there's distraction in excitement with the imminent race.

"Well wait til the race ends. It'll be quick."

Silence. Wonder. Thoughtful expressions. Is this right?

"Right, okay. Wait till it's over. Check his tickets. Get security after the race. Sit down. Wait. Nothing we can do about it anyway."

They agree. The race starts. Time lapses. They're engrossed with betting results. Bing's lifeless eyes stare, his old frame sinks slouching.

A half hour. They're men caught between the excitement of adrenalin in the bet, and the dignity of duty in their loss, letting their friend sit in his seat at the track, in sudden warm death.

The betting settled, and the police arrive with pens. "What's the gentleman's name?"

"Bing."

"I mean his full name, first and last."

The old boys look at each other.

"What's Bing's name?"

Silence. They continue to look to each other.

"What's Bing's name?" is the question none of these old boys can answer.

In a less official tone, "Well how long have you men known Bing?" They look at each other.

All their attention on the weight of this. They calculate. One answers, "Forty years."

"You guys know this guy forty years and you don't know his last name?"

They just look at each other. Smirks amalgamate with concerned glowers.

"Well is Bing his actual first name?"

Forty years of Bing in the circle, and no one—though they may have it buried deep in some dementia—recalls his full name.

They can't help but laugh, restraining themselves in the absurdity of their senile oblivion, with the gravity of his departure. "We're old. We're confused. We forgot," one says, hoping for mercy from the policemen's stunned scrutiny.

How the quest for money can intrude into life like an unseen fiend, consuming living, hearts, hours. The quiet yet glaring warning that "... *those who desire to be rich fall into temptation and a snare and into many foolish and harmful lusts which drown men in destruction and perdition,"* goes unheeded. *"For the love of money is a root of all kinds of evil, for which some have strayed from the faith in their greed, and pierced themselves through with many sorrows."*

A great big gambling monster is a big part of the household where Sherry grows.

At home Sherry feels misplaced. She feels injured and ill informed, and the reaction to her world erodes her emotions, moving her on a search. Roman Catholic Sundays, library hours investigating world religions, reincarnation, self-proclaiming prophetic mystics professing answers from trances, astral projections, meditations—these and other probes consume her reading.

Boys' invitations for dates are welcomed with a yearning for attention and love. She falls "in love," goes steady with two upperclassmen two successive years. She is sought for. Yet both "loves" decide to leave her for more promising ventures in girls.

She sits in aftermath in her teenage world alone, on jetty boulders by the Great South Bay in a new feeling of rejection. Rejection stuns her with that old pain. Boats enter and exit.

Brown's River inlet. Gulls shriek. A buoy horn blares. The bay's waves slap with rhythms. She wishes the water would wash her life away. She neither understands nor accepts this pain found in rejection. Bemused in deluded self-examination after the second rejection—she feels more discarded than betrayed. The pain of rejection seems to seize her. One week she's precious, valued; the next she's worthless, feeling an unflagging ache.

"Greatly beloved." That's how the scriptures tell it—through the voice of an angel to Daniel on the banks of the Tigris River, in the center of a great query toward God. Our incredulity makes us ignorant. Our ignorance makes us unstable. All the varied shades of brown—all of humanity—through centuries remain "greatly beloved," sought for on the world's shores.

Bought, ransomed, cherished—keys stripped violently from the hands of the prison keeper, God's message to the human race remains, "greatly beloved."

What does an adolescent know of being "greatly beloved"? God is patient, forebears to be sought for, waits like the father of the prodigal; seeks intensely—reaching, calling, like the shepherd of the lost sheep. What does a six-teen year old girl know? More than a four-year-old? Depression blooms like a cumulous thunderhead, shadowing, ominous, arriving like dark brown weathered glass found by the sea. We strain to see through dark glass.

These feelings of faded worth are like a murky ghost. She walks through forlorn months after each of these dismissals—somehow maintaining grades, somehow keeping social demeanor. Cries become appeals for future light.

A new prospect opens. A youth retreat seems like some-thing that holds promise! She rounds up friends for a week-end. The girls are divided into groups mixing with unknown church kids. Young leaders are eager to pass a flame. Ses-sions through the weekend bring Sherry and friends to what she calls "closer" to sating that missing piece in her life.

Focus is brought to the last hours of Jesus' life. Emotions come with nebulous realization of a God that loves his cre-ation. That link for a sixteen-year old girl—on what to do with that incident in human history, on how to fasten that his-torical event to living—now—without accent on significant application to the resurrection and transformation, on the pos-sibility of a new heart, new Spirit—that unattended link is hard for a sixteen year old girl to connect. Nothing lasting changes.

Rebirth found in an intentional response to follow Christ daily when the call is heard is vital in a sixteen or a ninety-year—old. It's a bond with God. The "heart of stone" sug-gests deadness, an inability to love God or people. One dis-abled to love is in spiritual disconnection, dead. But the "heart of flesh" revealed in the scriptures is sensitive. It's new life, foreshadowed in Sherry's life, that's able to relate to "true light." God places a "new Spirit" into the believer. He is working, timing, coming. He's planting, watering, plowing, seeking, preparing.

THE PAST
Memory, the past.
The sound in a scent, the touch of a sight,
Something subtle touching some sense—
A taste in time suddenly brings them there—
Down
Dragged to those
Sunken stones
At the bottom of the sea
Where vivid words are chiseled, still images.

Memory. The past.
Just a song, or a scent,
Something soft touching some sense—
Four chords suddenly bring me here,
Clear, up from depths with sounds of stringed instruments
Pumped up with air to breathing surfaces, clear,
Then higher in air, farther to clear heavens—
Hot air balloons bursting,
Rising full with color.

Memory. The past.
We search pages for an old page of pain,
The weighty warm ache of memory,
A photograph, and old stone,
An unforgotten gist,
An ache of pleasure.

Grade twelve arrives, 1974. Daunting adulthood and hopeful notions of the future grow serious. Sherry and Cliff have begun daily ten-minute attendance-homeroom together before classes through high school. "Hello" greetings are cordial, but detached. Enrolled with four hundred seniors, Sherry is sewn more into the socially well-known.

Youth retreats continue—mixes of kids of mixed interests, with a gamut of sincere inquiry for God, some with notions of knowing God, with the elemental hunt in discovering themselves and human nature heightened. They're young thinkers in a spiritual drift, neither evangelistic nor Bible studious—an emulsion with troubled homes, bothered minds, regrets, even desperation. Few are achievers, most unremarkable, stereotypes—whatever that might be—reflective of the 1970's—adolescents finding footing in a fast changing, complicated America.

Sherry's invited to be a group leader, ones who'll speak a twenty-minute message to an assembly of sixty kids, preparing with nervousness.

Through these weeks she and Cliff grow into a revived friendship, as in intervals of middle school. From mere passing in school halls, in town, familiar only from muddled memory of puerile middle school play and crushes, Ringolevio on sunny days, they're scarcely aware of one another. Except by nodding single word smiles in homeroom, they're more like strangers.

She's the good girl branded by physical attractiveness, unreachably impossible in his estimation. She's that quiet secretive girl boys apologize to after using foul language in her presence, whom some nick-name "the ivory soap girl." She wears a melancholy countenance, sometimes laughing with sparks of radiance. He has never heard her speak at length—ever—even in childhood—never heard a complete sentence. Shy, wary—even teachers find her a mystery. She's a non-participant in group discussions, an ambiguity.

A rehearsal practice speech—to ease stage fright before the weekend, facing an audience of six—she begins. Cliff is unexpectedly taken by an enchanted mesmerism, finding her expression riveting. How did this girl remain hidden so long?

Why have I never opened any exchange? It's a discreet quietness—a serene well—undetected, a reflection rendering this mysterious allure—non-physical, almost unearthly. How did she escape his attention these years? A veiled sparkling grace spills out in unexpected boldness—expression sodden with unpretentious humility—swinging wide open a gateway to his curiosity like sunburst through a gap in clouds! This is Sherry Pisani? He's attentive in spellbound attraction. This girl is entirely exquisite!

It takes a week. Real courage is a leap seized while fear paralyzes; it's a stride taken despite the power of apprehension. He understands this. This nerve is not a courage mustered up inside, enlisted into his conscience, but more of an unruliness.

It's less bravery, more daring foolhardiness. He calculates that while it's not imprudent, it's wise timing—stepping out with carefree audacity during this anticipated weekend. It takes a week of thinking and planning: I'll say, "I'm crazy about you," he imagines.

He approaches—her red sweater, blue jeans, blonde tresses, captivating purity. Neat, natural, clean—her jasmine smile greets him in the big retreat house kitchen. He remembers Ringolevio. Go for it, he thinks. "Can we talk a few minutes Sherry?" He lets it spill.

"Of course."

Stunned for five seconds—"Maybe in the chapel? It won't take long."

"Okay." A smile.

He quavers. "In fifteen minutes?"

"Okay."

The chapel's a small room—chairs, a cross on a wall, a statue, a Bible. They're alone. Thoughts bounce from fear of an appearance of brazenness in his intention, a possible barefaced effrontery in social incivility, to the awareness that something socially leveling, equalizing resides. It's the setting—this chapel—breaking the delusion—his own diminished esteem; something renders them parallel on a plain as simple children again.

He arrives surprised to find her there before him, observing in inquisitiveness. A seat, a deep breath. "I have to admit I'm thinking about you a lot this week."

Her smile dissolves a mountain of hesitation.

"I am wondering—I'll be straight." Now there's no turning back. Panic: he's crossed the Rubicon. For a moment he attempts to scramble thoughts—to retreat and say, "It's a nice weekend isn't it?" or "Can you help me with my speech?" or "What's your favorite food?" or anything more trivial, but then wonders how bizarre that would seem having this formality in the chapel—to say something mundane. This meeting in this setting becomes promissory. He's obligated to finish.

"Would you?" Here it comes—just say it—the voice in his head—say what you're thinking, he resolves: "I'm a bit of a short nobody. Would you ever consider going with somebody like me?" Pause. "I really like you—even once when we were kids. I have to confess Those Ringalevio games? I know this isn't the best way to ask."

He feels heat of blush in his face. But the thought arises suddenly that—perhaps—the chapel is the best place to ask, however it's asked. She smiles, looking at him, hands together between her knees.

"You don't have to answer me now. I had to ask." He smiles back at her. It's as if time takes on a personality, a third person presence. An awkward half minute mocks them. "So, let me know. Okay?"

She nods through her smile. "Okay."

"Why did you come here early?"

She shrugs her shoulders through that continuous smile.

On a stapled brown paper wall—bulletin board of a sort—where messages of inspiration are written in blurbs, read daily by kids, some designed for specific readers, some coded, he later discovers Sherry's handwriting, cryptic to others: I like you even if you're short. SP.

He's fallen into a dream, wants to leap with joy. This acceptance is almost implausible. He feels a keen romantic elation, with an eager caution not to impair anything.

This is their beginning—unromantically romantic.

Months plod into that 1975 spring, near graduation one afternoon they lie beneath a huge linden tree in tall grass on the fringe of the Bayard Cutting Arboretum, on their backs gazing up. A sunny day approaches its end. Months are behind them—drives together, eating out, walking shores and paths, sitting in her living room, eating with her family... He's grown bolder and just lets the words fly out of his mouth: "Someday I'd like to marry you."

A span of silence—maybe a whole minute. His eyes are closed, waiting in uneasy wonder for her response, both fingers tightly crossed.

"I do too."

"Really?"

"Yes really."

He feels nervous happiness, somewhat dazed—the same euphoria after the chapel talk. "Wow," is all he says, grinning, eyes opening. "Wow!" He looks at her. "We're meant for each other?"

Eyes still gaze up through branches. The scent of brackish waters of the Connetquot River traces the air, distant geese honking, the horn of a passing train. Wordless quietness lasts minutes.

"Do you want kids?"

"Yes. A lot of them," she says. "And I want to live in a quiet place, a big house, a rural place, near the sea. I want to bring kids into our home—ones who have none, kids with nobody to love them. I always wanted to help orphans." She dreams with this decent hope in her heart, a dream that creeps stronger as time presses her closer to adulthood.

"I've thought like that too. Not sure of 'a lot,' but I've thought of doing that."

"You have?"

"Yes. *Oliver Twist* started me on that."

"Really?"

"Really. Charles Dickens—that book." He wants her dream to become his. "I like it. I will work hard. I'm not afraid to work.

We can do it." Wind. Birds. Geese. "I'll do anything. I love you."

Two minutes of quietness endure in shared blushes of discovery. She rolls to her side and puts her hand on his face, turning his eyes from the high limbs, to look at him, to search for candor in his face. She wears her innocuous smile that lifts one cheek always upward. She loves him, she thinks, aware that he's still stunned in disbelief. She turns back to look through the linden, beyond into June's blue. "Me too. I love you too."

"So this was a good talk we're having."

"It is."

The beginning of a storybook, she hopes. And there is a God, somewhere, maybe near. They linger in the arboretum through the late afternoon, doze into sleep, awakening as the sun sets.

SOMETIMES FAIRY TALES
Sometimes fairy tales are forged.
Twilight's curtains close.
Bloated moon rises in rose
from repose
Over this little city,
Waking, whitening, laundered
From sleep's capricious dreams—

Eastward sitting on rooftops,
kneeling between steeples, chimneys,
Over streets where curtains close in windows,
Streets where hands hold, where feet stroll.

"The moon! He's angry! Agony!"
"No. The moon is laughing."
At dawn, whitened from sleep's capricious dreams.

These two find in surprise their moon again—
Like a grouse in gray, perched in boughs,
a child's face, adrift to sleep.

BLUE TRANSFORMATIONS

Years fly into another blue June day, that longest day, summer solstice; the wedding day is crowded with promises. Five years have passed since that afternoon beneath the linden, eleven since those awkward Ringolevio days. It arrives at the end of college years, years in aircraft manufacturing where she works in a logistics department, where he works on the shipping docks. The waiting engagement ends; wedding bells ring into a new blue sky. Dowling College ball room—she is adorned in traditional white. Sounds of simple strings of a blue grass band, and after months of planning, it arrives. She's twenty-two, laughing, scared, happy.

She's waited for him to settle down, waited out during his drifting travels through western states, Canada—in rides begged hitch-hiking, drives in jalopies—aimless wandering, a restless year-long chase moved by fearful capricious rummaging, delving for adventure, searching, the semi-typical "I have to do this Jack Kerouac thing." She's waited in patience for him to settle down.

Marriage begins in a tiny apartment—a two-hundred year-old structure—historically a chicken coop—part of the century old farm and stables of the Vanderbilt estate in Oakdale—later converted to one of the flats that evolved into an artist colony in the sector of the college.

They can finally live their "Wouldn't it Be Nice" dream of living together. Five years of life's fits, confusion of school, bike rides—merge into this clearness. The marriage vessel sets sail on a honeymoon in Newfoundland—winding farm roads, coastal fishing villages, forest paths.

"For now we see through a glass, darkly; but then face to face: now I know in part; but then I shall know even as also I am known." 1 Corinthians 13:12

God's varied valued gifts of the Spirit in 1 Corinthians 12 deflate beside the defining features of love in chapter 13. The closing of that celebrated passage reveals Paul's note of truth that in our mortal conditions there is a fuzzy understanding of the ways of God. Blurred, ambiguous, hard to grasp—the vision is merely emergent, scarcely clear—as in a strained look through dark glass, hazy glass—or even as in straining our eyes to see clear reflection in dark mirroring glass. The great apostle employs the metaphor of childhood—that unclear, unsophisticated time of mortal life where knowledge and notions are sully, indistinct. *"...But when I became a man, I put away childish things,"* he affirms in verse 11.

Expectations in responsibility that come with adulthood glare. Our mortal temporal sojourn here on our extant planet—however many years—as we're visitors, is a brief journey through, but a stay that demands perseverance in faith. It's like fleeting childhood. Afterlife with Christ will one day emerge wholly eye opening, as understanding is maximized in adulthood. Love will last, "never fail" there. We're unknowingly yearning—in the arcane parts of our lives—for that life, that last clearly polished vision. As for faith and hope—faith will be consummated then, and hope achieved; both swollen into things that become unnecessary, exhausted vehicles, spent needless tools as we arrive to that life, the awaited appointment that rewards the faith and hope, a marriage union with Christ, what's most hoped for in this final shape of life—heaven with Christ—seeing Him lucidly, as we shed the fallen, juvenile, broken state. *"The greatest of these is love."* Love continues.

At the most easterly point on the continent—Sherry finds on a Canadian beach a rarer fragment of blue sea glass from an earlier decade—one likely broken from an old medicine bottle—a curious soft-edged slice—thick, dark, refined. She holds it up to light glimmering dimly through, expelling imagined seasons of darkness that have sequestered there on the shore.

"Look. Blue. I found a blue piece."

"Let's see."

She hands it to him.

"Rare?"

"I never find them home." Her squinting grin flickers like the child's in her Fire Island summers.

"Nice."

"Yes," she says.

He watches her. "You're my lucky find," he says.

Waves tumble. Rhythmic resonance insets further into recesses of memory. This piece finds itself in her pocket to carry to her collection, a redeemed piece, removed from its own broken stormy story—a piece once part of an intact whole which held some sort of curative remedy.

A February Sunday morning, 1981: they lie together in their loft bed looking at the ceiling. Cliff's working the night shift, attending day classes at school. "I'm bored to death with church," he confesses openly. "Don't want to go. Same rituals, dead homilies. Pointless. I have a lot of school work."

There's no protest. She feels the same. She feels—maybe prematurely—that marriage is a bit of a disappointment too. Eight months—but marriage hasn't brought the fulfilling bliss naively anticipated. Something's missing from her life. She identifies an overriding emptiness; but in her young view of things, she won't speak about it yet. It's a huge emptiness that crammed its way into her heart.

Her Roman Catholic practice now comes to a halt. Their observance by choice from childhood through adolescence-when both resolved to revere the God they believed in, through the only practice they knew—despite the lack of family ovations—until now—is edited completely in early marriage, ending in a bewildering awareness of emptiness they've acquired, paradoxically in religion, in the practice they assumed would be the answer and in their living; ending here in a crowded busy existence that has no room. She doesn't refute God's existence, but admits a hypocritical measure—her Sunday rituals are dutiful—mere compunction, duty driven. It's grown into a conscience soother, a means to compartmentalize faith into a closet rather than the living room of her life. Pursuit for God is not the hub, but a broken spoke in the cyclical motion of living; the reverence is an old photo tucked in a memory drawer of innocent ignorance of formative years, never having been the framed painting above the mantle. Thirst for truth and the ache for rapport with God falls as a white, forgotten, inaccessible piece of sea glass into the assorted white glass jar, scarcely the treasured "pearl of great price" prize drawn from the bucket, placed in the little pocket for keeps.

The gradual descent from the search for God spirals through these years; it slopes downward from when her heart was smitten in sincere quest, when wills inclined in a chase for truth and meaning, savoring practice of religion—no matter how far or how the pursuit for God seemed to provide mere scraps to satiate. The indefinable ache for God froze into cold numbness. If God or truth could be discovered, it was not through religious ritual. He is not confined in a building or denomination. She settles the matter. They both harden their sentiments against hypocritical mounting wealth, esteem of wealth, show, and artificiality they perceive in church. Clouded, soured, they mutually surrender, relinquishing exploration through observances, fleeting contacts of "peace" handshakes with congregants assembled as strangers. It's strangely precise that at this time—like a dream—an alteration stays on the threshold.

***

Moses spoke in that ancient desert. He got his directions directly from the Director. One outward custom was for the people to create little tassels on their garments. God wanted a blue thread through the tassels. The observance's purpose was to remind them to observe God's commandments at all times, to shun the destructive power of sin, to separate themselves from other people of their ancient world, to detach themselves, elevating themselves—not in pride, but as exceptional people that belong to God.

A thread in blue is a reminding cue of the sky's blue—heaven, where God's throne is, where all good emanates—the unlimited power, mercy, grace—eternity itself.

And then in that old wilderness journeying, covering the ark of the testimony, they used badger skins, "*and spread over that a cloth entirely of blue.*" Also, "*on the table of showbread they shall spread a blue cloth...*" (Numbers 4). Aaron and his sons, priests, descendants of Levi, wore garments made of skillful precision "for glory and for beauty," with specific conspicuous color: "*And you shall make the robe of the ephod all of blue.*" (Exodus 28)

"*Over the table of the Presence they are to spread a blue cloth and put on it the plates, dishes, and bowls, and the jars for drink offerings; the bread that is continually there is to remain on it....They are to take a blue cloth and cover the lamp stand that is for light, together with its lamps, its wick trimmers and trays, and its jars for the oil used to supply it.*" (Numbers 4) These and other inclusions of pure primary blue speak of things eternal.

Reminders are important for forgetful humans who tend to forget God's commands, power, goodness. It's often the outward practices, the observances that actually do help us remember His constant presence, unconditional love, and perpetual pursuit of us. It's those memorials built that bring us remembrance.

Blue is a primary color. The adorning tassels are constant.

Blue refreshes our consciences into that infinite dimension into the invisible world, symbolizing the unseen which we're called to "walk by faith, not by sight" toward. We see the reflection of that sun-filled daylight sky in cerulean blue—on the sea. The tide comes in; the tide goes out. The sea level falls; the horizon extends—in blue, vast deep indigo, perfect sunlit sapphire. We see it in chicory blossom, the mussel shell, the robin's egg, the forget-me-not, the periwinkle snail. We see blue, then remember that God wants to be remembered, not forgotten, always remembered. True blue—sometimes moody, melancholy, downhearted—sometimes cerulean, azure. We remember that God never forgets. Forget me not! We remember that God remembers. We forget that we forget, that we need to be reminded, taught that we must remember. We forget. God remembers.

Blue has come to suggest mood—plausibly arising in the disillusionment of early marriage, the disenchantment of post—adolescent youth. Humans inherently become blue, then contest the blues, become down-hearted, melancholic, and all without understanding the human malady. We're ripe for transformation; we're blue, with morose blues. We're desperate for something definitive, for truth untainted, true blue.

***

The night shift brings Cliff a new array of co-workers. Two of them are Christians—he was warned about when he was on the day shift. "Jesus Freaks" in 1981 meant anything from Mormons to Jehovah's Witnesses to Hare Krishna people to Moonies to high pressure religion salesmen, to phonies looking for money, to ambitious religion builders, to people who like to sing with guitars, to long haired people with no frills, to seemingly genuine followers of Jesus, ones who want others to "know" Him.

He observes for months, distrustfully disengaged from direct conversation; but he listens, sniffing vigilantly like a hungry fish on its predator's bait—curiously peering like a devil's spy—suspiciously, yet yearning for something true blue, hoping that there was truth, yearning for pure blue. It's in spring 1981 when his challenge-questions erupt. These two Bible reading "freaks" do provide some answers, and also "some things we just don't know" responses. The skepticism tussles.

"Isn't God too good to damn anyone?"

"God is merciful. He bases salvation or damnation on one's acceptance or rejection of Jesus Christ—the only way," Vinny says. "We learn how good He is, and how needy we are."

"But my sins are not that big, why worry?"

"Any sin separates a person from God. And sin enslaves people. It hurts people. It brings eternal death, and God's remedy to bring sinners to Himself is Jesus Christ, the bridge. It's following and loving Him which matter most," Chris replies.

The sounds of forklifts, smells of metals, mold, and dust collected on crates stacked and long standing, murmurs of night workers, and sounds of hardware scales and distant radios scrape and crackle in the florescent lighted spaces.

Questions nightly: "Why does God allow evil? What if I just try to do the best I can? What about all the phony hypocrites? What about all the other great men who say they have the way? What if I wait until I'm older? What about human suffering? Where is God in that? What is sin? Doesn't His book have contradictions? Do I have to make it public? What must I do to be saved? How can I be sure of it? Why is God ruling a world that is all screwed up?"

He arrives home from work regularly after midnight, curiously enthusiastic. A revived fondness toward spirituality has him waking his wife, explaining, reading passages, reporting. She looks at him with those affable green eyes—inquisitive, wondering, listening, unsure, even wondering with suspicion: "Have you been taking drugs?" It's this strangeness, this novel excitement. "Are you brainwashed?"

They begin to read New Testament passages they've only

heard aloud from pulpits, but never themselves probed. In these page-turning hours, exploring, hammering in aim to hit a nail's head of discovery—it's like lights suddenly turn on. It's as though in a dream—a light beams, blazing their intellectual and emotional judgments with a revolution dispersing darkness. It's a result of a quest for light, a finding from seeking; and it all seems to occur with subtle suddenness. The conclusive verse withstands inspection: *"For God so loved the world, that He gave His only begotten Son, and whoever believes in Him should not perish, but have everlasting life"* (John 3:16).

May 1981—a first ever attendance in a protestant church service. Sherry marvels that people here are actually friends with each other—talking, laughing—are not strangers passing through a Sunday duty, but share a sociability unlike the quiet suburban estrangement among people in her childhood parish. There's a frankness of their plainness and unapologetic human fallibility which seem to eliminate hints of hypocrisy.

That spring transports light into her life, a striking compliance bringing moral senses, assurances of truth, right, wrong, and awareness of her own sin. She's roused to a remorse, an understanding that she needs recovery from a numb existence, to be protected from a Godless eternity. She is roused in conscience to this ostensibly urgent desperation for Jesus.

She concludes that Jesus Christ is who He says He is. In a stream of summer reading one evening, discovering in the eighth chapter of Acts the story of the baptism of a newly enlightened Ethiopian man challenges her with her questions about personal choice, as opposed to infant "christening." This Ethiopian's eyes are unveiled to the surprise that Jesus Christ is the fulfillment of the suffering Messiah found in Isaiah 53, inscribed over seven hundred years before His advent. In that flurry of resolve on that warm June 1981 evening she announces, "We need to get baptized!"

"We do? Again?"

"Yes. Like in the Bible. See? We should. We didn't understand when we were babies. John the Baptist baptized adults. They understood they were sinners. It's a baptism for repentance."

They cross the bridge to Fire Island. In deference to the scriptures, in the rushing foam of the Atlantic, they baptize one another, sealing decisions amidst rumbles of ocean water. Two new souls, aware that in laughing triumph they've dived on a new venture—with a long road of before them.

BLUE BROKEN MUSSEL SHELLS

They shine on the wet shoreline—
Blue fool's gold for sea glass seekers
Who search for the piece of great price—
The blue, amber, red piece of sea glass—
The shard of farther history,
The painful traces, slivers of another time,
Wound makers healed dull, softened by sea,
Fully colorful. You can spot them,
The sea glass seekers, that is.

They slowly stroll in bare feet, heads bowed
Crouching searchers. Bend, reach, lift, look—
They learn they've been lured by a beach devil's deceit,
Crustacean skeletons—
Blue broken mussel shells—
From the ripples of man's first fallen brokenness,
When he was sought for by Him who valued him
who was lost in Flimsy death,
the remains.

The strong fingers of storms and tides comb, comb,
And comb again, raising old sea glass
from beneath time's sand—
The weighty stones sink.
Frivolous sea glass rises, repeats rising,
to their shapely colors,
The pellucid to pearly white.

Transparent lusters appear
Above the crystals of quartz, gravel, and stone—
Gifts from the past—human past.
Fingers excavate, sort, search.
Nothing resurrects like the combing of the sea—the tide,
The storm, combed through smooth—
Soft shards of thousands of yesterdays,
Even a hundred years—shards separated from shells—
Preserved ruins of the labors of man,
Old ocean worn, sea broken glass.

NEW LAVENDER

What seems to be happenstance is a part of divine order.

What is sometimes esteemed luck, is really God's nod. Chance? Fortune? Misfortune? Accident? God is in total control of everything, every little thing; and the history in scriptures prove this repeatedly.

Ruth gleaned in Boaz's field. Joseph was sold to Ishmaelites. Peter sailed into port without a catch of fish at the hour Jesus spoke at the Capernaum docks. Job lost everything in one day. Love permits pain. God blesses, and God permits pain to bless. "God is love."

The many narratives are many evidences of a sovereign author designing every rising and falling action, every climax and resolution. We can live with perfect peace at every turn and stop in our driving, walking, working….through life. We don't obsess over deciding between what to eat on a given morning; but when we pray for wisdom, care, and direction, we can decide—trusting His control—forwardly with the big matters, trusting His leading, confident there's no time lost— ever—in the prescribed waiting periods for His children.

Moses' forty years in Midian ended on time. We live by faith, not by what we see. After the last drop from the brook Cherith dripped and the last raven left the last loaf for Elijah, he left for Zarephath with no evidence of stumbling through unbelief in God's provision, forbidding his situation to come between himself and God.

We don't see the sun through dark heavy clouds or gloomy watches of night, but it's there in the heavens. We can't measure God's involvement by the appearance of situations.

Darkness never overcomes light. He is never uncaring no matter what our senses tell us.

Weeping without consolation beside a grave can't give back that banished loved one. Sorrow gouges a deep hole. It leaves an ineffaceable scar, but of course there is healing. But we never get over our big griefs, because we are never the same after passing through our darkest waters, hottest fires; yet we can rely on the heavenly doctor's medicine and surgical tools so that we can continue in grace, optimistically confident that all things are functioning with perfect precision for His planned good.

God longs to lead us. We need to follow—at His paces. God requires that we trust His leading. It's the resolution of the story our impatient selves are after, but we can't hurdle ahead and read the story's conclusion with any satisfaction, without first treading through every event in the plot. We can't fast-forward without experiencing the full sum of the plot twists, and the climax. We and God are writing our and part of His big book of the ages.

God's story, His story, history reveals this long saga of a long suffering God dealing with stubborn, or blind, or dumb as sheep people who have always behaved these ways through the centuries because we—the largest part—remain dead set on believing and demanding that we are the main character, that we are the subject of the main theme, that we center the principal theme of the history, aiming to make it man's story.

Sherry's conversion is her biggest life renovation. It all begins in May, lilac blossom time—the time of splattering of lavender—in sync with their purchase of their first home. Lilacs symbolize first love and romance in a sudden bloom, a strong scented bloom, signifying spring, Easter, resurrection. The ancient Celtics believed lilacs to be magical flowers. It's the flower's blatant fragrance. In old Russia a tradition has family hover lilac over newborns, to bring wisdom to their futures. In the United States it's the New Hampshire state flower, significant of a hardy plant, a "Live free or die" people. And in some scholastic domains the flowers come to signify confidence for graduates.

The lavender of lilacs, the blue-red-white of lilac, one flower with medicinal uses, including soothing depression, built itself an attraction singular in sight, smell, and touch through centuries. Van Gogh and Monet both included these in paintings. Whitman penned free verse "When Lilacs Last in the Dooryard Bloomed," lavender colored lilacs serving as the symbol in the life after death narrative depicting Abe Lincoln's demise. The color lavender—no one knows exactly how, when, or where—but is common knowledge—somehow it began and grew, spreading to cultures, to define caution, a sign to be cautious, careful, attentive.

Sherry stands in the deep property that May day, amidst rife fragrance and lavender lilacs dappled in green, with calm contentment.

"It's nice."

"It is."

"Quiet here."

"A lot of trees. I love lilacs."

They talk. It's a house, a purpose for shelter and thoughtful investment. It's pretty. That's enough. To these two, choosing a house is not a matter to spend too much time with. It's the first and only walk through. They've heard of obsessive searchers who look at a hundred homes, indecisive. Nonsense.

"We'll take it. We'll buy it!"

"Wow. That was easy. Okay, we'll set a contract date."

It's 1981. These naive twenty-three-year-olds are buying a twenty-three year old home, the first and only one they appraise—no bargaining. $29,990—the asking price. Five rooms, one bath, garage. May, lilac time. Center Moriches,

Long Island—farmers, fishermen, merchants, commuters, civil servants.

She's easy to please. In October they would move into this modest place that needs a lot of work, an edifice between a creek and a river near Moriches Bay, beside a wooded preserve on a quiet south shore street, decades before urban sprawl would begin to reach eastward. It's her time of significant change, her rebirth from death to life, from self to Christ.

Views of horizon stretching fields of hyacinth magnify places in the growing fields of the world in this pigment called lavender. Hyssop also bares in purple-blue, and with a lighter variety in lavender. After King David sins, in Psalm 51 he expresses a hope in God's supreme forgiveness. *"Cleanse me, purge me with hyssop, and I will be clean; wash me, and I will be whiter than snow."*

In Exodus 12 the hyssop flower is arranged by God to be used at Passover to paint door frames with blood in order to detour the death angel. In Leviticus 14 hyssop and blood are for ceremonial washing for leprosy, the emblem of sin. In Numbers 19 hyssop is used for cleaning, purging—as a small broom. It's used repeatedly for transferring cleansing blood of the sacrifice to the sinner, to souls of humankind accepting God's remedy.

His hyssop—blue of the eternal heavens, purple of the royalty of Christ, tinges of purity in white: blue, purple, and white—all leveling into a lavender linking connector—hyssop—the applicator of the vaccine—pure perfect blood of Jesus Christ, applied symbolically to the darkness of sin in man. Hyssop—the lavender brush that washes.

This hyssop recurrently points to the atoning death of Jesus, the substitutionary, once-for-all bloodshed, the propitiation for reconciliation; and the applied blood is the braced, embracing bridge. This beautiful branch reveals itself in John 19 when the thirsting Jesus is offered a sponge filled with sour wine on hyssop, putting it into His mouth, just before dying.

Foreshadowed in Gethsemane, wrestling with His Father's will, He prays, "*O My Father, if this cup cannot pass away from Me unless I drink it, Your will be done,*" with that cup denoting the price He would offer to pay our debt. The cup of God's wrath and judgment, the sour wine applied to the recipient of God's anger, Jesus Christ, by means of hyssop, applied during a torment of death—the cup of woe all human souls deserve to drink because of our guilt for sin—that cup becomes the cup He voluntarily drinks, because it was His Father's will. That drink—the wrath could have been lifted from the sinless one, if He chose; but then that chosen suffering for our rejection of God would not have been removed from our destiny, had not the Son of God swallowed it for us. This wine from these grapes, the grapes of God's wrath, is transferred to His lips via this hyssop, concluding in His final breath.

Jesus withstood a revolting death in our stead. He drank what we should drink, metaphorically swallowed in His thirst what we should in ours. God ordained this hyssop to avail itself there at the crucifixion divulging His former intentions in the ordinance and ritual of the old covenant. He ordains this hyssop, fulfills His will in the new covenant through Jesus.

God's love for man and hatred for sin saturate the scriptures.

Why this bloody religion? It's God's method to demonstrate His justice and purposes. It's what He has chosen.

Ultimately, it's the blood of Jesus, not of unblemished animals as on the door frames of Egypt, or in the tabernacle or temple, or which Moses sprinkled with hyssop; it's the blood of Jesus Christ of the new covenant that finally soothes God's demand for justice. Ultimately, as He cried, "*It is finished,*" His agony on the cross pays the fare for the cost of our rebellion.

We see lavender in the hyssop. We let it remind us of our link to Jesus, of the drink he volunteered to drink for us.

"*Cleanse me with hyssop*," David prayed in agony over his own noted careless sins—adultery, murder, lying, pride… in emotional and spiritual torture from the weight of his own admitted transgressions. Cleanse me with the blood of Jesus! We can cry, delivered with the same confidence and faith in God's love, system of justice, and willingness, and power to pardon.

"Wow we're buying a house. Neat!"

"Beautiful."

"I feel like it all happened so fast," she says with a smile in the sunny fragrance of lilac. "We're blessed."

For months they work on floors, trim, sheetrock, spackling, painting, interior, exterior… remaking their place. Weekdays they commute together forty miles to the aircraft manufacturing plant. Before 1982 lands, just before Christmas, Sherry conceives, declaring she knows the measure of time on one given day that conception began. "I don't know how. I just know," she smiles.

Thirty hours of labor—Sarah is born in the heat of August—nearly ten pounds of beautiful, healthy girl. Sherry's hopeful that one day God will bring her girl safely through her own difficult corners, learning herself to rely on Him. Like a mother with her infant, when God almighty puts a weighty challenge upon His child, He puts His own hand underneath—supporting, sheltering. In Isaiah 49 He vows, "*See! I will not forget you… I have carved you on the palm of my hand.*"

Lessons she learns these years are pronounced around God's unfailing provision. These early days are conspicuous in shortages—always a daily dependence—for the basics to be met—food, clothes, medicine, fuel. She resigns from her position at the aircraft manufacturing company, filling days at home with reading stories, songs, walking to the creek to feed ducks. She resolves to allow God to fill their house with the music of His presence.

"Look at this." Sherry hands Cliff an open magazine. An

edition of *Decision* magazine in 1982 reveals facts of open doors to countries in South America for orphaned children available to adopt.

"Now? You want to do this?"

"Well maybe we can look into it? It doesn't happen that fast anyway."

In May of 1983 when the lilacs bloom again—she finds the name of an adoption counselor. At their appointment they sit across this desk, Sarah on their laps.

"So you have a child by birth, and you want to adopt?"

"We always thought of helping kids who have no one."

To this semi-retired consultant in his sixties—Sherry and her husband, looking like two teenage kids—it seems a little premature, presumptuous.

"It's quite an expense to adopt. You have the resources in place? There are legal fees, for both countries. Transportation costs, agency fees, medical costs."

The economy rebound has only begun. Their fifty-dollar fee for the hour consultation leaves them cynical in their zeal, realistically challenged by what accompanies accomplishing something like this for God. It'll entail a contest to their faith, an enterprise that could daunt anyone, a cost to be counted; it won't be a walk in the park.

Exiting the office, a question on this man's expression, he says, "Well you have a healthy child. You're young. You can have more, right?"

"It's not so much for us. We want to give an orphan a chance."

"Very nice. That's noble. I will never discourage that." His tone, Sherry imagines, suggests he views these two as naïve, idealistic, and to a degree he's right. "Consider these avenues I've suggested. Know what you're up against, and the best advice, if you're serious—take the first step. One step at a time! Otherwise it may all seem impossible."

That afternoon she tries not to waver or lose heart, not to

abandon what may be a lofty wish, but to hold the seed conceived in her heart, planted even in childhood—not yet birthed.

In June that year, sitting in the windy yard—Blue Jays in trees and soaring gulls higher—she considers all that is lately enfolding: she's conceived again. Revealed by sonogram to be a girl again, this one's expected in March of 1984. She feels pain, but doesn't think too much about why—this disparity in sensitivity—this time, or whether some pain at this stage of gestation is sometimes expected.

It's been two years since her conversion. Her faith is still green. With gratification, thinking of her present rivaled with some of her past, those earlier days of new conversion seem sugary; but now it seems diluted in anxious waters of care. That early phase God seemed close, now she wonders if she's wandered. She resists the doubting of how real it all is. In Job 29, the legendary sufferer probes, "*Oh that I were in months past.*" She sees marginal fruit in her life, or what she's expected.

She doesn't "feel" the fruit, doesn't notice in self-examination growth evidences: "love, joy, peace, patience, kindness, goodness, faithfulness, self-control." It is a dry interlude in her life.

Our human consciences aren't as sensitive at certain times.

Zeal cools. We question, "Is this happening? Or are opposing voices accusing? Or am I seeing this correctly?" Sometimes asking, "Have I been remiss in devotion? Allowed an idol to step between me and God? Has my affection allied with something other? Have I allowed the love of the world to replace the undivided engrossment of heaven? Is my heart divided? Did I allow the testing of deferred hopes, postponements, delayed expectations to invite a slow departure? Am I impatient? Love of God ought to be foremost. Can I keep that aflame? Has God retracted? Have I withstood prideful self-righteousness? Am I putting confidence in myself rather than reliance on God?

A withdrawal from the way she trusted "in months past," has come to her attention, and she can't just pretend, hoping without exploring. I should ask His help with childlike humility.

He promises to fulfill His plan. "*Now to Him who is able to keep you from stumbling, and to present you faultless before the presence of His glory with exceeding joy, to God our Savior, who alone is wise...*" (Jude 24).

At the end of August, after weeks in exhaustion, she suddenly begins to bleed, believing the worst. "Go directly to Brookhaven hospital emergency room," the answering service voice says. "Dr. Jean says he'll phone the OBGYN on call there, and he'll come himself in the morning."

On the way they stop at Grandpa and Grandma's carrying sleeping one-year-old Sarah.

An overworked, young, foreign gynecologist places a stethoscope to Sherry's abdomen, searching, listening. He moves it, listens, moves it repeatedly. Shaking his head, and in broken English, "Dead. No heart. You have miscarriage. You will miscarry by morning. All you do is wait." He exits, unenthused.

"Call people to pray Cliff," she says in a burst of tears.

Quarters in a pay phone: church people, prayer chain, family, radio ministry lines. In the dark hours—amateurs to the faith—they pray, turning pages, hoping for a miracle. Is this a promise? Joshua 23: "*Behold, this day I am going the way of all the earth. And you know in all your hearts and in all your souls that not one thing has failed of all the good things which the Lord your God spoke concerning you. All have come to pass for you, and not one word of them has failed.*" She clings to this as a hope, bypassing the second part, the part like many other promises that hold conditions.

It's Sunday. When morning lightens, Dr. Jean arrives. The moment he places the stethoscope down he finds a clear heartbeat. "Sounds like baby is fine. I don't understand," he says, continuing to listen.

The attending night shift nurse, having listened to their hours of praying, wells with tears.

"We prayed all night," Sherry says.

"Well I don't know what happened last night, but there's a definite heartbeat now. I want to take a sonogram—take a look. You'll stay one night. In the morning we'll take a look."

After the sonogram on Monday Dr. Jean says, "There's a condition called placenta-previa. Don't know if it has some-thing to do with not hearing a heartbeat on Saturday, but the sonogram shows the placenta is attached too low in the uterus, Mrs. Schrage. That causes bleeding—not constant, but intermittent. You have to rest—complete rest—a couple of weeks at least." He is emphatic. "Somehow you need to force yourself to get complete rest Mrs. Schrage."

For months she does her best at resting, with no problems, besides the fear. Cliff comes home from work and manages things. He and Sarah grow indissoluble while he's home, allowing Mommy "a lot of rest so baby sister in her belly is happy."

December comes. She awakens from sleep habitually in the dark hours of early morning. She sits with her Bible, pray-ing with an uncommon prompting—opening inexplicably to the references to Job each night. December progresses. She begins to retain water, her body swelling to a degree that she can't put shoes on. It seems she isn't passing water.

On December 29 she calls the doctor.

"Come at three o'clock," the receptionist offers.

She drives alone. Sarah has a cold. Better if Cliff remains with her rather than shuffle her to family. She leaves dinner in the oven.

The nurse takes Sherry's blood pressure three times. She leaves the examining room. Sherry hears her knocking on the adjacent door. "Dr. Jean can you come here right away!"

The doctor abandons another patient. He takes Sherry's

pressure, and without consideration says, "Mrs. Schrage we have to get you to University hospital immediately."

"Can't I go home to rest?" She cries, thinking—her one-year—old, dinner in the oven, normal living.

"Your blood pressure is so high you could have a stroke or a seizure. You've gained ten pounds in less than a week. You're retaining water. You have to get admitted to Stony Brook. They have the only neonatal intensive care unit in the county. The only way to cure pre-eclampsia-"

"What's that?"

"It's toxemia—the only cure comes in delivering the baby.

Your body is having a negative reaction to your baby is the best way to explain. This is very premature. Only twenty-six weeks, and the baby will need a lot of attention. I will go and explain to your husband."

"My husband isn't there."

"I don't understand."

"He's home with our daughter."

"You drove here in this condition?"

Tears flowing now, "I didn't know."

Fearing frightening her further with insisting on an ambulance, the nurse calls Cliff with urgency to immediately admit his wife into Stony Brook. Sarah is taken to family.

One from the OBGYN staff is waiting with a wheelchair: a flurry of engulfing hurry, new faces, transits, questions: "Can you see clearly? Do you have a headache? Do you feel like you're going to pass out?" Sherry panics.

They proceed with a catheter, intravenous, attachments to monitors, attention to numbers, blood tests, conference between doctors. One nurse is assigned exclusively to Sherry. She is lain on her left side, as a depression of blood pressure on internal organs befalls this position. Dr. Jean is not affiliated with University Hospital, so Dr. Davenport, the chief of OBGYN—a poised expert in her mid-thirties relieves Sherry's anxieties, explaining the dangers, caution they'll take—watching, waiting, balancing with decision between interest in the unborn—duration in the womb—and the interest in Sherry—keeping her organs functioning. "One hour at a time Sherry," she leans in with a forbearing sensitivity. "Your job is to rest. Stay calm as you can."

Having received her records, Dr. Davenport is attentive to the seriousness. A specialist from the neonatal critical care unit enters. "Mrs. Schrage, If your child is taken early, and it looks like this could be imminent—noting measurement in the sonogram, she'll weigh just two pounds. At 26 weeks she'll need respiration, incubation, feeding tube... She'll be too premature to suck. Very critical for weeks." He stops, and with a human smile says, "Have you chosen a name for the baby?"

"Rebekah," Sherry says.

"Beautiful."

***

There's a favored lavender sea glass that remains rare, some more replete in the Canadian Maritimes and the Northeastern United States. The common knowledge in the sea glass world is that this glass was first fabricated with manganese, a bleaching element in the process to make glass transparent during the World War I era. This particularly clear glass—dated—is transformed into lavender over decades. The lavender turn of glass is an evidence of the beauty created of some things in time, in aging. A lavender piece is hard to find, one Sherry's never found in her twenty-six years. Scarce are pieces of seventy-year-old storm-tossed glass marvelously tainted into lavender. It's one of those childlike secret wishes, longed for discoveries—a piece that when found will be certainly smooth, old, lavender.

LAVENDER
Favored hue, lavender—
Scarce as silver,
Loved more than blue,

Pervasive through blooms—
Tone of Innocence
Scents in silent stillness;
Tone of devotion—
Silent, lovely,
soul cleansing lavender.

GOLD REFINING

When one encounters a beautiful, Christ resembling character, we know the journey she has made isn't beside a
blooming blue sky, June path of beauty only; but rather a jag-
ged, stony, stormy one where gusts from blow to their limits,
where briars cut and impede, and where slithering beasts
threaten. Faith grows in storms in the spiritual atmosphere,
conflicts with antagonistic elements. Spiritual giants are
formed on roads of joy and sadness, trouble, tears, and peace,
danger and misunderstanding; wind, rain, hurricane, and
balmy sun. Fiery gusts grow hot and blow from hell, and
God's voice may say, "Go in. I'll go with you."

***

The smoothest, loveliest, most resplendent glass is made
in the stony ocean surf where it's beaten and refined.

Nothing in the gentle sandy bay, no glass is transformed
into shapely colorfulness while sequestered in safety—it's for
those left surrendered to the tossing billows.

Christ-likeness is a journey of joy and sorrow, healing and
pain, victory and falls, friendship, persecution, misunderstanding, false accusation, tribulation, and calm.

God meets us in the severest heat and tossing process of
refinement. Faith grows in the turbulent tribulation of the
tossing surf. God speaks his truths and secrets there.

BROKEN FROSTED SHARDS

We're broken frosted shards of history—
Some of us—
washed up glass on shores,
having decades' long voyages—
once feeling cast as refuse
into storms—later
waking up on a coastline
awakened into gems
transformed by sand, stone, foam—
the more furiously violent
the more beautifully smooth,
color-softened, refined.

The winter solstice passes; darkness moves into 1984. Five days in concentrated scrutiny and meticulous care lapse. As Sherry's blood pressure drops, she's transferred from the delivery room facility to a regular hospital room. The longer Rebekah can remain in the womb, the safer for her.

The move to the new wing on the gurney takes her into the elevator. The nurse wheeling her in steps back to grab Sherry's bag of belongings, and the door suddenly shuts, leaving Sherry inside alone, recumbent on wheels. Having grown accustomed to hospital life, she's relaxed enough to laugh rather than panic, and she shifts into simple laughter. Alone in a busy hospital on one of several elevators, in a twenty-floor building, she loses breath with laughter, separated from her care taker whom she knew would eventually reconnect. The elevator stops and starts. It goes up. It goes down…. a few minutes pass with Sherry lying on this gurney unattended. Her laughter increases into hysterical laughter, so much that she is afraid she will be unable to explain to any who board the elevator about what has happened, where she belongs, why unattended...

In time they reunite. When she's comfortably situated into her new room, and the blood pressure monitor is reconnected, it reveals a significant drop. The nurse is baffled. "How's that?" She giggles.

"A proverb says 'a merry heart does good like medicine.' I think it means laughter! That was hilarious."

"Not yet." The nurse smiles.

In the morning of January third, Sherry's blood pressure rises again. Dr. Davenport says, "Your kidneys are failing. There's signs your organs are beginning to fail. We're scheduling you for a C-section tomorrow. It's serious Sherry. How does January 4th sound for a birthday?" This self-assured physician moves close to her patient, holds her hand, looks into her eyes, explains with efforts at non-medical language; and she waits for questions. "Your husband should go home to sleep."

Cliff reclaims Sarah, goes home for rest. He rocks his one year old in the rocker. Upset from the disruptions of her contentment in routine, Sarah's restless. Holding her until she falls asleep, he himself sleeps until 6:00 PM when the phone rings. A hospital voice, "Mr. Schrage, your wife is being prepared for emergency delivery. You'll probably want to come right away."

Sarah is quickly taken to Grandma and Grandpa's again. He drives to Stony Brook. Once he enters the surgical ward, he's intercepted by personnel, and his wife is wheeled aside at the operating room.

"Cliff if anything happens, please whoever you marry, make sure she loves Sarah and Rebekah, and please, remember—name her Rebekah. We agreed. Right? like it's spelled in the Bible—K-A-H ending."

"Stop. You're going to be fine. I don't get this, but you're going to be fine. Please be fine. I love you."

"I love you too."

They are parted. Doors open—a sterile white brightness flourishes from inside, movement of masked faces in blue scrubs. Doors close. Her husband stands outside until a staff member leads him to a waiting room to sign forms. Full of thoughts: Rebekah's coming. We're all separated. Life was nice, but now we're scattered. Emergencies are cyclones. Family life was pleasant in our little house sailing smoothly. What's going on God?

She is anesthetized into a deep sleep, unmindful of what will follow.

***

Gold. There is a long and tedious course of process in its refinement once it's found. It's worth something when drawn out of the mine, panned in the river; worth more when reduced, honed into bars; more again when refined into coins; increased in value yet more into jewelry. What a fiery slicing and sculpting the gold goes through to increase its value. The more it's misshapen, formed, extracted, heated—the larger its worth. God's metaphors help us to "be still and know that" He is God. His words recharge trust, purpose, power—no matter what part of the perpetual process we're in in His bringing us "forth as gold."

Common knowledge in the sea glass seeker world survives—that much yellow-gold sea glass originates from depression era tableware—a valued collectable; it comes from specialty glass, ornamental glass, pale yellow milk glass, old Vaseline jars. Trifling amounts of yellow glass were produced. It was rarely discarded as it was mostly ornamental, special. Some is "sun colored," originally clear glass turned pale yellow because a selenium content in past glass making processes reacted with ultra violet sun rays.

Yellow-amber sea glass—even much rarer than lavender in the tones of gold—signify success, enthusiasm, happiness, power, even victory. These scarce colored pieces collected, usually small, Sherry has never found.

God trusts us with our suffering. He gives a vote of confidence when he loosens us into a fiery trial. It's a paradox: He is the one who gives us faith, and He has faith in our reactions of faith in Him—to give Him deserved honor and attention in our testing. He allows us this peculiar opportunity to endure.

He gives His grace.

Certain metals are capable of undergoing more than others, and after the refinement, they yield more strength, durability, value. God intends to get all He can out of us. He wants to retain possession of us through these processes and blessings. He wants our lives to tally dividends for Him, for people, for the world. He aspires shining lamps filled with His oil on tables, glowing cities on hills, lights in storms. He wants us formed into sun colored, shining gold.

"Can't I do with you as this potter does? Says the Lord. Look, as the clay is in the potter's hand, so are you in My hand," Jeremiah 18.

"Fear not... I will help you, says the Lord... your redeemer... I will make you into a new threshing sledge..." He comforts His Own in Isaiah 41.

The fishing boat threatened with waves; Jesus was asleep, and His friends in terror claim they are perishing. Didn't He respond, *"Why are you fearful, O you of little faith?"* and didn't He finally rebuke the storm, causing calm on that sea? We learn in the storm. We focus in the flare-up. We cry out loudly to Him in the tempest.

In the scriptures gold is found in Havila, Ophir, Sheba, and Arabia. It's used for money, jewelry, offerings, misused for idols. In scripture it's often a metaphor for refined saints, purified faith, the redeemed. Of course we're not literal gold, metal, fishermen, or clay; but lessons are for us in reconciling with his classroom demands until we're finished here on earth, beyond our sojourn, moving on. Gold—it seems a perpetual process.

There's a constant tension at play in this life, this world— bodily, emotionally, relationally, spiritually. We can't be surprised by sudden shifts in weather.

Another part of the process in the factory, another challenging climb around the ascending bend in the road, another fire in the valley, and we can't forget the glass process.

It's fire that makes it useful in its primary creation. It's brokenness and patience in waters of time that make it fair in texture and color, cherished in rarity, as in lavender and yellow, hues that speak of femininity—all grown up, in refinement, elegance that is delicate, precious, bright, rare.

***

Rebekah is separated by C-section. Sherry is stitched closed, and all seems well until there's hemorrhaging observed. The misplacement -earlier noted—of the placenta since conception is the culprit.

Sherry's raced back into the operating room, and Cliff is entreated to sign for an emergency hysterectomy, which is hoped end the bleeding. A signature grants the surgeons permission to take away his wife's dream of bearing children. This relinquishment of this hope floods him with new unforeseen emotion. What happens in Sherry's discovery when she awakens to this loss so early in her youth?

After this second round in the operating room, she is returned to recovery with close observance of vital signs. Wait, see, monitor—until it is soon noted that the hysterectomy, intended to remedy the profuse bleeding from her uterus, has not aided in clotting the hemorrhaging.

A third entrance into the struggle: still unconscious she's wheeled into the operating room for Dr. Davenport and her team to see if there's something they've missed—an untied artery, a crushed vein… wherever this blood flow originates at this point.

Through an hour of physicians probing, exploring, blood seeps continuously profusely. Units of AB+ are transfused into her body, replacing units that are exiting. At this point Sherry acquires DIC (disseminated intravascular coagulation). Her blood loses coagulation entirely. There's no clotting factor.

Platelets are depleted. Medical staff refer to DIC as "death is coming."

One last effort. This medical team visibly anxious—their

twenty-six-year-old patient, a woman with a husband and babies—and before the induced sleep, alive still with a thin measure of hope. Sherry's yet again moved into the OR with a faint possibility that this fight isn't over, they open her again, pack the entire bleeding cavity. Hope, see… minutes.

Once DIC arrives into a victim's body, blood seeps completely unleashed. She bleeds from her nose, ears… multiple orifices. Sherry's end is pending– the staff realizes. She is clamped, stitched again, placed into a trauma suit—a squeezing apparatus cased tightly around her legs and abdomen to keep whatever pumping blood that remains in the circulatory system flowing primarily in her organs.

Wheeled now into the intensive care unit, fallen into a coma, nurses are directed to keep units of blood transfusing into her veins. A twenty-hour stretch will ultimately mount to 102 unequaled units. Each minute wavers in uncertainty.

Her husband calls people who pray. Some arrive in the dark hours of the night to sit in the waiting room. Having found a corner for an hour in the first-floor chapel, he finds an open Bible on Psalm 91. He revisits a story in the gospels—a woman troubled with twelve years of bleeding, who is able to penetrate throngs of humanity pressing around Jesus. Fallen to the ground, she reaches, touching the edge of Jesus' garment, finding instant healing.

"Let her live. Please God help us!"

Strangely, a quiet "John 11:4" impression finds its way to his thoughts. Unknowing, he opens pages, finding at the beginning of Lazarus' resurrection story, Jesus' declaration *"This sickness is not unto death, but for the glory of God, that the Son of God may be glorified through it."*

"Is this You God?"

All night her condition becomes a buzz overheard through the gossip in surrounding wings. One young university intern finds Cliff in the waiting room. "I heard of your wife's condition," he says. "I've been praying for her."

"Well thank you."

"You may not understand—don't know if you're a believer, but I think I'm supposed to pass something on to you. I wouldn't ever be so daring if I weren't confident I've heard God speak to me—and I don't want to offend."

"Tell me. Please. I believe."

"A scripture from John 11, *"This sickness is not unto death, but for God's glory, that the Son of God may be glorified."* I believe your wife is going to live. I'm out on a limb here—don't even know you, but I believe God is saying she will live."

"Wow! I just read that."

"Really?" A smile. "Now that's confirming"

Within that hour a caller broke through the phone at the nurses' station, from a small group of friends praying in the night hours. "We believe God's shown us a promise: *'This sickness is not unto death, but for the glory of God, that the Son of God may be glorified through it.* John 11.'"

"Three times. Same verse! Thank you God."

While procedures accumulate in the ICU with looming peril—surgeons, anesthesiologists, RN's, a cardiologist—all attentive, somewhat crammed into the midnight room, one of the assisting OBGYN's is released to verbalize: "Mr. Schrage, the situation with your wife is not good at all. It's very grim, and I have to say it's very unlikely she will survive. I'm sorry to have to say this Sir."

Cliff doesn't know how to answer this: unresponsive, awkward, but then feels he should say, "I don't want to sound crazy or like I'm in denial or something, but I believe God will give us a miracle. Maybe you believe, maybe not." Cliff is reluctant to add details to his confidence. No one responds. No one, respectfully, would dare contest a strange hope at such a distance of time.

The bleeding somehow stops, and in a meticulously topsy-turvy slow pace, vital signs begin to make a turn. Platelets are transfused. Sherry ascends from the coma, but for days remains on a respirator. It is a baffling supernatural phenomenon.

A week passes—a setback: infection in her cavity develops; there's fever, and she's unresponsive to antibiotics. She's forced to return to the operating room—another hurried visit as fever heightens and organs are wearily stressed. There is a strong sense that there's a battle. The large mass discovered which caused sepsis infection through her body is removed surgically first, then doctors continue doses of antibiotics. She is forced back onto the dreadful distress of a respirator.

Again, a healing process inches onward. A friend reminds Cliff of the story when Jesus once found Peter's wife's mother lying sick with a fever, touching her hand, the fever leaving. Anything positive is received.

Another week passes. Rebekah staggers on her own uphill climb in incubation on the eighth floor. Dad visits daily, talks to her. She's entangled in the monitoring and feeding wires and tubes which keep her frail life growing forward.

Days pass and another sudden scare ensues when Sherry's given heparin, a blood thinner. It was never before known that she's severely allergic. Her immediate reaction to heparin obliges the staff to send out another "code blue!" through the ward. Respiration stops. Heartbeats stop. Staff members scurry; she receives the urgent resuscitation and survives another near fatal knockout. She's put on the ventilator again for another week. It seems like health progress has moved in a pattern of three steps forward, two steps back.

On the morning after, she writes of her experience: "I felt I was rising fast—going up. I saw faces I don't know. It happened so fast—soon as I got that heparin. I had this feeling I'm not supposed to die yet. Saw one face I knew—Gary's. I think God showed them to me like I had a purpose yet, like He has people for me in the future—some purpose in the future. It was so real, so vivid!"

After these intense weeks in ICU she's finally moved into a regular, less intensive room. It would be another two weeks until her home coming.

Because it's against regulation to bring children to ICU, Cliff says, "We have to bring Sarah up to see you now. She's so sad."

"Please. Yes."

"I got her coat from the closet to bring her to Grandma this morning, and she reached up and pulled your coat sleeve—your burgundy corduroy—and she just started to sob, and she kept crying, 'Mommy!' I couldn't help but cry too. I know she remembers you."

"Can you get her now?"

It's hard for them to predict how their daughter will react after all these 'no children in ICU' weeks. Sherry braces herself, knowing Sarah needs her mom.

Later in the hospital room when Sarah sees her, she puts her head down averting eye contact. Sherry—gaunt—just doesn't look the same, especially in a startling, strange setting. She takes minutes to move closer to the bed, toward Mommy.

Daddy lifts her, walks toward Mommy. He leans her, lowering her toward Mommy's drawn, different face. At first this one year old spins her face away, over Daddy's shoulder, squeezing him, in terror. He backs away holding her. Sarah relaxes.

"Talk to her Sherry. Your voice may do it. It's Mommy Sarah!

See?"

"Hello Sarah. I missed you. It's Mommy. See? It's me sweetie."

"She's relaxing her grip."

"Oh it's been too long." Sherry's eyes fill.

He sits on the bed beside her, holding Sarah. Minutes pass.

Sarah looks at her mommy. She reaches then—from Daddy's arms, down toward Mommy, and lays her head on

Mommy's shoulder, burying her eyes there. This reunion with her eighteen-month old restarts their attachment.

Seven weeks of care in Stony Brook University hospital bring her into February. Cliff's work days have been sparse in attendance at the airplane factory, with days home with Sarah, with Sherry on the 18th floor, and Rebekah on the 8th floor, and the depletion of paid sick days brings the family to financial straits.

Sherry's homecoming is applauded, but one year old Sarah's grown unfamiliar with Mommy. Life has been upside down for this one year old. The disorder of routine, unpredictability in her days have ushered some fears. Coming home that sunny February day brings the three of them back to a replica of the way life once was. Rebekah remains in incubation in neonatal ICU.

Two weeks of easing back into home life becomes a mending for the three of them. Sherry has weekly doctor visits. Cliff is taught to dispense daily irrigation of wounds The beginning of March arrives, and Rebekah reaches her state of criteria—readiness: four and a half pounds, no need for oxygen, ability to maintain body temperature, and drinking by bottle. With special demands—a lot of rest, warmth, head covered, feeding in three-hour measured increments—even to be awakened for—the awkward difficulty of this tiny one's homecoming is augmented by both her and Sherry's frailty. No matter, home feels like the most placid place.

In April Sherry hears wheeziness in Rebekah's breathing. Dr. Ginsberg guesses asthma and prescribes meds. By April's end the wheeziness worsens. "Bring her to Good Samaritan Hospital. She must have pneumonia."

She is placed into an oxygen tent for two days, then sent home; but a perpetual wheeze remains, with a tense struggle for air, obvious discomfort, a fussy exasperation that is constant through May. This all cuts into her sleep. The "pneumonia" is dubious. Dr. Ginsberg suggests an air conditioner.

Somehow with this edgy, tight-rope walk with Rebekah's

continual crying, labored breathing, sporadic sleep, and difficulty eating, she survives a month.

On June 12th Sherry puts her in her crib as usual. An hour passes; she awakens, gasping, crying. Her lips are palpably blue.

Dr. Ginsberg: "Bring her to Good Samaritan Hospital."

With limitations to diagnose clearly, after two days, "We need to send her to Stony Brook," a physician's voice orders.

She's returned to the place of her birth thirty miles away.

Poor oxygen intake requires her to be put on a respirator, and dispensed a particular drug to bring her to a deep, near coma sleep, a kind of paralysis while doctors have room to investigate. The cardiologist concludes her heart is strong.

After days, evaluations reveal a trachea problem; but she would have to be moved again—via ambulance—to Montefiore Medical Center in the upper Bronx, seventy miles away. Even modern Stony Brook University Medical Center is insufficiently equipped to scope closely into the trachea of an infant.

After a long separation from Mommy in the ambulance, where a respirator can't be administered, but rather a manual oxygen pump is manipulated—through slow traffic and a time consuming misdirection, the ambulance arrives, Mom and Dad following in the family Plymouth.

The trachea-bronchial airway specialist Dr. Rueben greets them in the emergency entrance, and straightway assesses that emergency tracheotomy is necessary immediately in order to prolong Rebekah's life. The trauma filled, alarming day puts Sherry into emotional anguish over the refreshed separation from her terrified baby.

After days of stabilizing, Dr. Rueben discovers through a bronchoscopy—a stenosis, a severe narrowing at the bottom of the trachea where the bronchial tubes meet—a birth defect—respiratory obstruction rarely found in premature infants.

Becky's airway has also been exasperated by swelling irritation created by the respirator tube.

Even this foremost New York City hospital is not sufficiently staffed for a respiratory case like Rebekah's. Dr. Rueben researches, discovering Dr. Frader in the United Kingdom, a specialist who's performed numerous successful surgeries on tracheas—old and young. Dr. Frader consents, arrives in New York, determines that Sherry's little girl needs immediate open chest surgery—where for the first time an infant this size would have a surgeon open her trachea at the juncture with the minuscule bronchial tubes leading to the tiny lungs, and replace with other tissue a patch—of a sort—allowing a widening, hoped for better access of air. She would need to be put on a heart—lung bypass machine. After surgery they'd hope for proper healing. "This will be outstandingly risky," he explains plainly to her parents. They assume confidence in Dr. Frader and Dr.Rueben. "There's a strong possibility this surgery could kill your daughter," Dr. Frader's words, spoken in an unforgettable British accent, looking into Sherry's tearful eyes. Watching their daughter's respiratory suffering has grown more unendurable by the day. They realize something radically extreme is needed. God doesn't seem to be performing any miracle.

"Why can't it be a cleft palate or something?" She let these words mutter from her lips.

With vigorous steps Becky's nurse Liz moves into the room with the head pediatrician Dr. Singer. Sherry is seated, but words jump up, "How's her last blood test?"

"Not good," he says, studying numbers on the monitors.

A sigh, with a slight sinking of her frame at this recent news, a last hope to either cancel or postpone the looming procedure, which seems like an experiment, keeps her staring at her seven-month-old.

Liz manipulates the arterial line, taking yet another measure of blood. Sherry wonders how amounts of blood could be removed from such a small, oxygen-deprived baby before it would be drained.

"Becky!" She tries getting her attention, calming her.

Plugged into a respirator by a tracheotomy, tubes and wires once again crossing and weaving attached to machines and monitors, makes her appear lost in cold technological estrangement.

She again recalls Dr. Rueben's explanation: "It's a tracheal stenosis, Mrs. Schrage, a severe narrowing at the bottom of the trachea." She needs to accept the truth, bidding the scalpel to open her tiny chest, to fix her. She doesn't like the medical, foreign language, perceiving that these medical personnel strain to simplify without condescending, carefully rearranging language. The image in her mind by medical illustration of her daughter's respiratory system is murky; but time—after surgery—measured in breaths, heartbeats, digits on monitors, shifts of medical personnel—all lapses behind.

I live here. We live here, beside this bed, she thinks, waiting now for major surgery, waiting for a turn. Her world is this—the preparation—elevator trips up, down—her second child's eyes gaping blue, trusting, yet in terror; the bizarre heart-lung bypass machine which would become her life; this delicate procedure; green garb hovering over her tiny treasure. She couldn't manage this, wondering why her innocent infant daughter must remain in undeserved suffering. She's reminded of scripture. *"For you created my inmost being; you knit me together in my mother's womb."* (Psalm 139:13)

She glances at her husband standing above. He looks at her tired eyes. Something inside softens. They look at each other long, steady expressions asking if something is more wrong.

Hand on her shoulder, he leans, presses his face against hers. "Love you," she says, placing her hand on his. She gestures with eyes that say she accepts his sudden warmth, looks back at her dying child. They gaze at her like mourners at a wake. She thinks, with abstract premonition she's learned to grow accustomed to, that this might be the last. They look for a long time.

A hospital administrator alerted to this family's situation arranges for them to stay in one of the Hospital apartments acquired for patients from afar—an adjacent building—twenty—seven stories above those Bronx streets. This kindness—at no charge—alleviates the apprehension of travel time and expense seventy miles from Center Moriches. Sarah, not yet two, bounced in a whirlwind since December, could be with Mommy and Daddy, as Becky's healing may be a prolonged grueling road.

"Oh my God, that's so nice of you, Thank you. Thank you very much."

It's afternoon, July 4, an hour before surgery. Sherry remains in the apartment with Sarah. She dials family: "Hello Mom.

They're getting the baby ready for surgery. It takes at least eight hours," she cries.

"Oh… okay… we will be thinking about you. Call us when it's over. Here, I'm going to give you Gary to talk. Very busy here. People coming."

"Coming for what?"

"It's the fourth. Our annual barbecue—in the yard." "Oh."

Sherry realizes they're alone in this one. None come beside her in these cruelest hours. There's an ambiguous understanding that even the lack of proximate human support is perhaps pre-arranged—the blunt purpose of learning His faithfulness and support, ascertaining God's promise, "I will never leave you nor forsake you."

Cliff laces through the turns in corridors and doorways toward the operating room. Inside the elevator's pause—climbing flights upward, beside two interns conversing-stethoscopes draped around their necks, he listens abstractedly to their greetings:

"What's doing?"

"Long one for me today—very full. You?"

"Me too. O.R. Seven-month old. Trachea. Not expected to survive." Heads shake. Cliff elects not to chime in. It's a mystery—why among such massive numbers and convolutions in hospital busyness—people dashing to and fro—this private chance intermission brings this elevator encounter, this earshot within the quiet pause.

The procedure begins. He sits in the waiting room, and the surgery extends through the night, and in the morning—finally complete—an unanticipated fourteen hours.

Sherry arrives with Sarah. Weary Dr. Frader sits with the family, and with that distinct London accent states plainly, "Mr. and Mrs. Schrage, the next twelve hours will tell. If swelling in the area persists, she will die."

A stunned numbness, then a contained burst of emotion from Sherry. Reality bores deeper. They would watch and wait. The tornado that has spun a second time this year keeps her clinging obstinately with God, having this atypical peace, assurance that something heavenly holds her together. This new wait-and-see begins.

It is often noted that human beings through history, broken and corruptible, fall into the documented record of atrocity, violence, rioting, and war. But what's undeniable is the other side—the God inspired efforts of the human race—this example seen patently in the sum of organized labor made for Rebekah. The expenditure of coordination, disbursement of funds, the unity of numbers of skilled hands, a flight across the Atlantic by an expert physician, and the compassion demonstrated for a tiny infant is hard to overlook.

There's a grand narrative found in the second chapter of Mark. Jesus comes with large crowds to Capernaum, enters a house. Throngs gather, squeezing in, bursting outside the door, hoping in fervor to hear His words. Four men carrying a paralyzed friend, unable because of crowds to get near Jesus whom they hope might bring cure, decide to get on the roof—carrying this crippled man. They dismantle the tiles aligned above where inside Jesus teaches below—and gently, cooperatively—they lower their friend lain in a stretcher, bringing him to his healing place, what may be his only opportunity.

The coordination of numbers of necessary skilled hands—and the compassion unveiled toward one significant life—small as it is, is remarkably conspicuous. A sin-tarnished world continues its spinning, waiting relief. Demonstrations of God's love are floodlighted into the fallen brokenness—in the waiting.

Evidences of His love are seen—through mankind too—as in the relentless, colossal effort for rescue of thirty-three men in a Chilean mine, deep inside the earth; as seen in the multifarious efforts of all NASA to retrieve three Apollo 13 astronauts back safely to earth after a failed attempt to visit the moon, as the whole world prays; as evident in New York City Fire and Police Departments who ascend flights of the Twin Towers under attack sacrificing to salvage hundreds from wreckage unlike any in history; or the hundreds of pleasure boats on the southern coast of England called to rescue thousands of stranded soldiers on the northern coast of France as Hitler's troops converge to subdue; or in the U.S. Navy's full capacity discharged into rescuing one single captain held hostage by four Somali pirates; or in the assembly of hospitals in New York, the arrival of a Naval hospital ship, and convergence of thousands of medical workers to assist in care for the onslaught of Corona virus victims. Whether it's three hundred thousand, three-thousand, or thirty-three, or three, or one—the significance is seen in the concentrated efforts from the God inspired side of mankind.

Exhibitions of the support seen in the human race, in its exertion to recover for the well-being of a small slice of its own, sometimes shows no bounds. Redemption for one single life shows there is good in the world, and the good is God—prompted, God-inspired.

Sherry's half day vigil advances. Everything cascades downward. Becky's skin darkens beyond blue, nearly black. Her kidneys disfunction—her body shutting down. Within hours, "Yes she is dying Mr. and Mrs. Schrage. Would you like us to remove her from the machines? Would it be easier for you to hold her and allow her to go?"

These words, a suggestion from some strange voice, hang in suspension of time for a long concentration. Sherry would have to answer. The news bearer is patient on this afternoon.

Through emotion, "I want her left on the machines, but I want to hold her."

She's placed into her arms. Her husband waits in the waiting room with Sarah who's unmindful of what's happening with her little sister. Two nurses volunteer their lunch hours—alternating intervals—to bring Sarah to the park and lunch, while the curtains are drawn around Mommy, Daddy, and Rebekah, struggling with acceptance of this farewell.

"She's in your hands God. I don't get this—any of this—but she's in your hands. Take her," she prays aloud.

Two hours. Cliff takes Sarah to the apartment to sleep. By morning Sherry sees a urine flow in the tube, a first indication of kidney function. A blood gas test shows slim improvement. Another test… more… then greater improvement. Healthful color steadily returns to her skin. A recovery somehow arrives, an observable return to life.

The chief pediatrician enters. News from evening physicians is brought to him—this totally unexpected ascent in this roller coaster experience around this child. Staff remarks, "Can't believe it. Doing great! Amazing."

Dr. Springer's words remain strong in her memory: "I don't know what you were doing behind that curtain, but this really is a miracle."

Rebekah later drinks a bottle, her eyes looking into Mom's, sometimes stopping her drawing—to smile—yet still confined to monitors, respirator, tracheotomy-silence.

YELLOW GOLD

Gulf of St. Lawrence glassy silence
Widens while we drift midway

Between islands whose calls of
Woodland ravens, crows, jays reach

Ears here—colliding from two sides
Across salt water miles while
We fish afloat adrift on our slim craft.
Sun falls yellow-gold. The gulf

Gulls fall, cry. Under the surface
Silence of life—herring, cod, crustaceans
Crawling fathoms farther.
Shells, bones of their dead loll

Amid man's rusted ruins:
Barnacled flotsam sunken
Amid colors—as sequins-
Sea glass—white to mauve, azure

To amber, yellow-gold
Century old,
Glowing tones
Of burning embers.

Sherry's health affects her stability. Blood work is taken repeatedly. Her body works to recover from the trauma of surgeries and intensive care earlier. Dr. Davenport cautions—the need for a year of rest for complete recovery. In 1984, having received so many transfusions, she's somehow shielded from HIV, but what has slithered into her system is Hepatitis C, the silent liver destroyer, a new strain the medical world has no cure for, and won't for another twenty-five years.

For the next three months they stay in the Bronx. Cliff returns to work at the aircraft manufacturer. Summer evenings he brings Sarah to the park, the zoo, Orchard Beach, Botanical Gardens, with quick trips up to the ICU to see Mommy and Becky, until, pulling his arm, "Daddy I want to go back to the park." The spread-thin life comes into rack focus for

Sherry this summer, while her strength declines.

Joe and Ellie Gugliotta come for a Saturday visit for support in late July. Nancy and Pat—mom and dad—on their way up for vacation, detour for a visit. Bills pile, yet provision arrives—like the multiplied fish and loaves, sometimes strangely seeming to replenish.

In the days after the major surgery Cliff's stepsister Karen volunteers to care for Sarah. Wishing for Cliff to obtain a family sick leave, Sherry prays, "God, so Cliff can stay here for support a few weeks, grant it please." Immediately after gaining approval from the personnel office, he walks back to his work station worrying about the income stopping dead. The lunch whistle blows. Sounds of rivet guns and drills hush. He grabs his bagged lunch, sits, opens. There inside with his sandwich and apple—hundreds of dollars in a tight rubber band from some mysterious anonymous giver—a simple hand written verse, "For your heavenly Father knows that you need all these things." No one was aware of his request for leave time.

Once on another August weekend with bill collectors lined up at the mailbox in Center Moriches, Uncle Rich pays a surprise visit at Montefiore Hospital. "How is the baby? How are you two? You're on our minds."

"Staying strong Uncle. Surprised to see you. Hardly anyone ever comes all the way in here. Thank you."

Small talk, with update on the long journey—difficult for Sherry to abbreviate because of the complications—brings Uncle Rich's visit to an end. "Here," he says, placing an envelope in her hand, squeezing his own over it. "There's a short note, a gift. Open it when I leave." He hugs them, exits toward that long maze of inconvenient hallways and streets, away. Sherry opens the envelope. Again, impeccably timely—a sufficient surprise, dollars—hundreds. Nights sometimes have a moon and stars.

Besides the reliability of God's grace and kindnesses shown, she learns another lesson: the awareness that culture inside a hospital is one of its own, with a wide disconnect. She comprehends, looking out the window down flights onto the street below. Eyes inside these wards have pupils laser-focused on sickness, injury, the decree of death. Relationships blossom with parents of other pediatric ICU sufferers facing life-long ailments or death; attachments with orphaned members like Janasia with AIDS, without a parent by her side, birthed by a mother addicted to crack cocaine, abandoning her to this; and Alex, a one year old undergoing heart surgery so he could hopefully live out his life—whose parents are steadfast by his side; and Jovan, premature like Becky, born with multiple birth defects, addicted to the drugs his mother was imprisoned to.

Many New York City souls no one knows of, alone in childhood. Coping—somehow in the grace God has to mysteriously provide, (It's harrowing to think of any existence like this without it) with needs they themselves are too callow to know—extraordinary as they remain completely alone. Sherry reaches, contacts each of these in neighboring beds, talking to them daily, coaxing them to grin.

Rebekah cries, a red-face from all the discomforts. But her cries, unheard in the tracheotomy which bypass vocal cords, are facial grimaces of screams, gasps, faint utterances, as though captured in film with volume off. But Mommy hears them—knowing by memory the sound of her daughter's voice. While discomfort accelerates—a needle, an adjustment—a physician, a nurse, a procedure—Becky's eyes look into Mommy's with naive inquiry, "Why do you let them hurt me like this?"

It takes an experience like this to consider another angle, His desire for us to know that He observes and intends the suffering "to work together for good." He hurts. "I'm here child. I know what you're enduring. I know it's hard to understand." Trust is hard in a broken world. But the hope remains: everything will eventually come to a falling action leading into a grand resolution. God doesn't miss appointments. He never arrives before His scheduled hour, never after. "Wait," is the cry. "*All authority in heaven and on earth has been given to Me.*" (Matthew 28:18) She believes. Paraphrased, "I'm the boss. I'm in charge!"

There's a world out there on those streets below—beyond—caught in the circular worries of life, oblivious—not at fault, but unmindful. There's a world in here that somehow develops an attentive alarm, a love of humans, attachment to humans who suffer.

"Can we take Sarah to McDonald's," Posie asks. "But it's your lunch time," Sherry says.

"But we want to. Let us," Liz adds.

Sherry tries to hand them cash. They refuse.

On each of her shifts Liz gives Becky three long daily baths, with all the tubes and wires attached. "But that's not called for."

"But Becky loves the bath. She smiles, and I want to make her happy. I'm happy to do it. That's why I'm a nurse."

One dark evening Sherry holds Becky by her bedside, while Marie holds hers after her child's recent heart surgery. Becky is smiling, reaching hands to Sherry's face. A passing physician steps aside, leans down to look, "Hello Becky! Hello pretty girl. What are you laughing about, ha? What are you doing?"

Becky loves the attention. Sherry smiles.

"You know when you're not here your baby gets a lot of little visits like that," Marie says.

"She does?"

"Always. Everyone stops by her bed to smile and talk to her. She gets very excited. She's so alert. There's something about that little one of yours. She's very pretty. That's why too."

***

The relief and pleasure of those simple words spoken become the acme of Sherry's day as she's continuously concerned, worried about those hours she's away from her Baby's bedside.

Summer passes. Rebekah remains in the hospital bed attached to the tracheotomy. Seven bronchoscopies come and go. Healing scar tissue slashingly forms repeatedly inside her trachea, blocking air. Dr. Rueben scopes, then probes with a laser, and little by little, scores away tissue, wary in the delicate painstaking procedure of not removing too much by increasing swelling.

A neurologist is summoned to observe if her periodic oxygen deprivation has caused new problems. She's administered new drugs. It's a summer-long struggle. There's an alternation from airway freedom to restriction and suffocation. The tide rises. It falls—July, August. Miens of terror, panic, suffocation—then smiling silent laughs, expressions of trust. Trauma for a baby, and torture for a parent.

When September arrives Sherry and her family are forced to surrender their apartment, and the seventy-mile commute to Rebekah's Bronx is on again. Jeremiah 8:19,20: *"Listen! The voice, the cry of the daughter of my people from a far country. 'Is not the Lord in Zion? Is not her King in her?' The harvest is past, the summer is ended, and we are not saved."*

With the return of the long drive, apprehension swallows her like a billow, submerging her into periods of emotional disequilibrium. Terror swoops with its talons. Tentative procedures—after the open chest surgery—stretch ahead like a black path through caverns. Images of hours by Becky's bedside flare with fear. The city drapes its towering temperament like a foreign country. This nervous convolution in Montefiore Hospital spreads surreal nightmares.

A pediatric unit, she imagines, is a site where these afflicted little ones are carried into the hands of caregivers—a kind of launching pad for those who expire—an ethereal post where this translation occurs, where tireless angels sent from the highest arrive to relay little ones home to rest.

She looks out the window, that same clear pane, down six

stories at the street's activity where all the world somehow appears festive, ambitious, forward; where every life moves forward. The planet rotates, revolves. Hers is frozen. No one waits for Sherry, for Becky, for her family. Incarcerated, thoughts assault her this afternoon. Despair. Evening—one of those windless humid summer ones—she stands staring through the pane of glass as she did a hundred times. They both stare silently, gazing out as nurses prepare their child for another procedure to open her airway.

Out above the towering concrete rectangular structures in the sky sable scattered clouds fusing with sunlight hover. Sun showers plummet colorfully unannounced like flocks of blackbirds. Her baby's frame lay grounded under the nerve—stunning drug, paralyzed again, prying her into passive panic visibly imprisoned in her eyes. As stiff as a doll, blue pigment blackening from scarcity of oxygen, eyes plead with alleged mistrust, wide with terror, cadent breaths enduring in unwavering rule of the respirator—always brushing against the dangerous edge of brain damage, or death.

"When's this going to end?" She mutters, hands clutching fingers.

She points over rooftops with child-like elation—a rainbow balanced in radiance, curved amidst ebony clouds and gold light. They look at one another. No words. A sacred timely hope calms the moments—a sign—maybe—some kind of byline from heaven, lowered, above obstructing high rises.

Later, the last hours of summer, autumn's equinox—11:30 PM, little Sarah is in her crib in Center Moriches. It's been a long day for all of them in the Bronx. Sherry—awake alone, finishes reading nonfiction, a story—a woman whose husband and toddler die suddenly, the narrative focused on how she triumphs over loss. Why am I reading a book like this now? she wonders. The phone rings. It's the head RN on the night shift. "Mrs. Schrage, Rebekah is not doing good at all. You probably need to come in right away." Her voice stings.

"She's taken a sharp turn. It's a matter of maybe an hour. I'm sorry."

She packs a bag for Sarah. They return to the car, accelerate onto the expressways, onto the Bronx River Parkway, straightway to Gunhill Road. Christian Radio's voice recites its routine late night Bible reading from those last chapters in Revelation. Chapters 19-22. "....*Then I, John, saw the holy city, New Jerusalem coming down out of heaven from God, prepared as a bride adorned for her husband. And I heard a loud voice from heaven saying, 'Behold, the tabernacle of God is with men, and He will dwell with them, and they shall be His people, and God Himself will be with them and be their God. And God will wipe away every tear from their eyes; there shall be no more death, nor sorrow, nor crying; and there shall be no more pain, for the former things have passed away."*(Revelation 21:2-4)

Pensive silence. She's tired, numb—like a soldier grown immune to constant sounds of war. They park—sleeping Sarah is carried, head on Dad shoulders, and they hurtle inside through the rehearsed maze, up an elevator, down three turns, through hallways, doorways, turns they've programmed. They merge in the passageways with Liz who's received her requested phone call—if anything should happen to Becky—while on her vacation.

Sherry recalls the last days of summer. September 22, darkness. Liz, leaving for vacation: "Becky's heart's grown very tired. We have to put her on Lasex because of all the fluid on her heart. Her heart at this point is the concern."

Oddly these last two days Becky's health seemed renewed.

She, Cliff, and now two-year old Sarah—spent most of the day at her bedside. They sat her up. She was laughing in her silent voice box, fascinated with her big sister. The soundless laughing made them wonder about humor—this human response—to an infant an indefinable untaught mystery. But it was laughter nevertheless, visibly loud, even though silent under gasps of a bypassed voice box in a tracheotomy. She was reaching, pulling her big sister's pigtails playfully in excitement. Sarah, understanding, endured a baby's playing in patience, sharing toys. The nurse puts her in a stroller. Grandma Nancy came in that day—her second visit. Again, there remained this apparent burst of energy, a happy notice- able reprieve from unabated suffering. They played, laughed. For the first time Becky drank an entire bottle for Sherry.

When it was time to leave in the evening, she didn't stop smiling. Sherry backed out of the room—looking at her daughter, waving to her from the hallway, hesitantly reluctant to go, wanting to stay, squeezing out every minute. There's something in the sweetness of her face that made Mom think she was saying "good-bye," even as she seemed at her peak in wellness. They drove home through the Bronx, over the Throgs Neck Bridge, through Queens, Long Island—the sev- enty-five miles home.

It is noted that—sometimes—the dying, young and old, in terminal illness acquire an unexplained mysterious revival for hours, maybe a day or more—a gift, it seems, a healthy surge that seems to come for an unexplained reason except for san- guine farewells endorsed from heaven. There comes this surge of communicativeness, eating, alertness—a sudden removal from what was perpetual tension and struggle, often raising denials in those loved ones encompassing. It can't be, Becky was doing so well.

They enter the ICU in the predawn darkness to the sight of her connected to machines, still, though they were told she was almost gone. Overcome with emotion, stepping outside for moments, the doctor comes out, "Mr. and Mrs. Schrage, we're sorry. We've done everything we could. Becky has passed. Her heart failed. Her body couldn't continue to fight anymore."

Sherry sits on the familiar chair beside the hospital bed, gently rocking her baby's lifeless frame, forward, backward… in rigid unison. The baby's face is serene, eyelids closed, while an inconsolable storm rages through Mommy. It's an unsettling picture of paradox—mother and daughter. "Becky come back. Please don't go!" The nurse can't comfort her. Dad covers his face. She refuses to be comforted. Grief, denial, and cover against this monster are heavy. The poignant travail found in disbelief groans. The yellow balloon, stuffed animals, musical mobile, The Psalm 121 frame, all become pieces to a puzzle.

She touches the blue scar expanded down Becky's tiny chest.

She touches her hands, runs a finger down the bridge of her tiny nose and touches her rounded cheeks. She buries her eyes in the cleft of her tiny neck and shoulder with tears. Last good-byes.

Dad leaves with a hospital administrator to sign documents, contacts the funeral home, calls Grandpa and Grandma who arrive at dawn to drive Sarah home. Given a little more time alone with her departed second born, Mommy gains a presence of mind—her daughter's now safe, no longer in pain.

They exit the building for the last time. The little body is moved to the morgue below. They descend the several white floors, entering the Bronx pavement, moving as though afloat beneath clear blue sky.

Sherry crosses an inactive street. Mortar and glass—the huge hospital rises above her this morning, she turns to give one long last look. She knows one window better than all, yet all of them possess the shining reflection of sunrise. Each window is a barrier of glass to this world, a world aloof to the world on the inside—each pane like candles as sun gleams on this equinox morning—painting hues of yellow gold.

Summer's gone. No walks along the shore, only this Bronx, pavement, shining glass hospital windows, the residue of a little hospital bed, tubes and sounds of evidence of a fallen world, a baby's silent cries. September 22 feels ceremonial, desolate. It's as though in this frozen moment on the pavement below flames on every pane are angelic eyes peering out, down; God's eyes see the ache and confusion on this bereaved mother's threshold of anxiety for tomorrow. She stares fixed at that one glass pane glowing yellow, burning with all the brightness of a summer gone.

Before turning toward the car with her husband, the bright flaming sunrise on the window melts into just another pane of glass, as the others. Her baby's not there anymore. This has passed.

North Bronx streets are quiet. Light traffic, muffled voices, a horn, a train's rhythm over Jerome Avenue, the initial momentum of a day yet to begin. The image of her propped-up daughter a day ago reaches for Mommy's affection. She says in a whisper, walking. "I will not be in fear of tomorrow."

They cross the bridge over the width of the mouth of the East River which trickles itself into Little Neck Bay. She looks toward the city of a million windows alight in yellow glass, reflection of sunrise. A wholesome Anger is there.

The sun shines in resplendent clarity into the equinox, another season. One season is gone, another season has come. Chapters. We're moving, she imagines, toward something promisingly golden. She feels the expected physical pangs of grief in loss—the difficult swallowing, the yawning, the chest pain found in mourning.

From a study of wolves—who when living in contentment, wag tails, even smile when they play. Packs can sometimes elevate in numbers over thirty, and when one pack member dies, all mourn for weeks, even revisiting the place where the death befell, and they grieve with mournful howling, all together with wilting, slouching tails. And if the fallen wolf were young, it is noted the mother grieves closest to the corpse.

Another snapshot of our fallen planet.

In the evening of that first day of autumn, unable to sleep, cleaning every corner of the house to ease nervous pain, worrying her daughter is crying for her as nothing is making any sense, crying to God aloud, Sherry says, "No one knows how I feel!"

A small impression seems to reply with quietness, bringing a degree of comfort: "I watched my Son die."

September 26 is a warm Indian summer day. She stands almost disengaged beside her husband, Sarah between them, before the grave .

"Mommy I want to go. Mommy please," the two-year old pulls Mommy's arm.

In cold months icy wind blows carrying broken clouds until sunlight suddenly bursts, a warmth comforts, light brightens like whiteness. In these hot months wind carries clouds and humid warmth falls under a coolness, cloud shadows suddenly rumple on the green, clouds cover with shade and many colors change—lavender, blue, silvers and golds transform. She gazes across the cemetery at locust and oak trees tossing in the hot wind on the perimeter. Family and friends depart in cars down narrow lanes squarely lain among rows of gravestones, and lanes strewn among fields of grass, a grid planned for future burials.

It feels like it's over. Her daughter's funeral. The three of them linger beside their ten-month-old's stone. Flowers, casket—she removes the photo, and they depart.

OPAQUE GLASS

Things get lost when they're moved. It happens in many translations. Messages in translations get lost, tossed, especially when moved from source to source.

"How can I say how I feel?"

"It's hard."

After it's told, it changes.

"Tell me what I said. How did you hear it?"

Time is a decoder too. Things get lost when translation is moved in time. Recollections wither and get frayed. Reading what's explicit often prompts reading between lines. We infer from what we imagine is implied—through what's read or said.

Things get lost in translations. Translation in prose and drama from one vernacular to another warrants expected liberties to be taken in the process, taken by scholars as they aim to make sense from one tongue to another. Conversion of poetry into another language is most vulnerable to bends and twists in the amendment processes. Corners are cut, losses surrendered in meter, rhyme, assonance and consonance, or other devices of sound; or sacrifices in meaning are forfeited to maintain a semblance of poetic resonance originally intended in the lyric. Or sometimes sacrifices that are impossible to avoid, to both meaning and sound, help meet in compromise. Some poets are persuaded that poetry has to stay in the language it is created in because of this. Things get lost in translations.

One year passes. It happens in the human experience.

Interpretations are hard in relationships. Sherry walks through her days caring for her daughter Sarah. She's numb, still ill, made frailer by grief, still seeing doctors to maintain balance and vigor. Grief brings a weight that wears the body out. The cumbersome barrage of reality: Rebekah her second daughter is gone now. Her ability to conceive again is gone, her childhood dream of bearing children, gone. Here's the death of a dream. She's developed a bad bronchitis. Her energy is low. Life's will to live has cowered like a fearful animal in a burrow. Living seems impossible, while the will to die is something to conquer, sometimes hour by hour.

"These will help you sleep," Dr. Davenport says, handing Sherry a third prescription. "Sleeping pills." Exhaustion and insomnia—it's a paradox. Weary wakefulness: an oxymoron.

This grief has intruded and become a predictably relational, marital separator, as in Frost's poem, *"Home Burial"* where the two—husband and wife—grieve differently over the death of a child, all because, simply, they are different. The husband in the poem soothes his pain found in loss, in his way; the wife in hers. Their differences converge in collision as the two emotionally diverge in distance—both converging and diverging—peculiarly at once. The famine of communication, with the intentional bewildering privacy, constructs miscommunication.

Something's lost in the translation from the depth of one's language of pain, to the other's attempt at understanding. And the understanding is hindered because the partner who's supposed to be understanding is himself or herself in need of understanding. And then there's that concept which itself needs to be understood.

That lengthy dramatic narrative in elegiac form is placed in a rural setting a century back—to an earlier America. Their baby dies, is buried in the back yard—common in bygone rural New England. From life to death, from the parlor in the farmhouse to the six-foot hole in the ground in the yard dug by the father, it is a brutal hostile pain. The wife buries her heart and mind in the loss, covering herself in it—as though in the ground itself, as sadly naturally as any mother would. She can focus only on her ache in this immense loss. His method is different. He holds at bay the agony, swims with intent to keep afloat from drowning, and provident in the total debilitation of sorrow, through tedium, by work, lost in activity, everyday triviality, which includes the exertions for survival and subsistence, the mundane diversions of escape. The balm for his emotional survival is a forced return to routine.

She says, "Who is that man? I don't know you... And still your spade kept lifting, lifting... You could sit there with the stains on your shoes Of the fresh earth from your own baby's grave, and talk about your everyday concerns... You had stood the spade up against the wall... For I saw it."

Her pieces of evidence to convince and prosecute, finalized: "I saw it." And there's the imagery of a muddy shovel, a tool for digging a baby's grave: it's the visible addition of a duty, something to be taken care of in the immediate.

The husband's response is summation of his behavior: he has begged her to let him into her grief, with a willingness at odds with an inability to help, but she was closed, choosing to be lost, not different from the natural mother who grieves in any time or culture, as the scriptural *"Rachel weeping for her children, refusing to be comforted for her children, because they are no more."* (Jeremiah 31:15)

The husband in Frost's long poem hollers: "I'm cursed. God, if I don't believe I'm cursed," finding himself human and helpless to contest the evil muscle of death, swallowing this pill of grief and angst over feebleness to assist his wife in hers. He has sympathy with himself, in this prison of predicament God and fate have abandoned him to endure. He's helpless to help. Their mutual loss is graphically exposed in their natural breaking apart, tearing asunder, undocumented divorce which is only hoped to be temporary. She won't allow him into her pain.

An extraordinary percentage of marriages that suffer the death of a child eventually fail. The bleak statistic is a blaring siren announcing its threat. The storm is over. This stark cold field in Sherry's heart is one she's never walked through. She is walking in winter. There are no flowers, only stones, snow, colorlessness.

One night the full moon drifts over Moriches Bay. It is bright.

She stands on the shore in her coat, down the road from her home, alone. The moon turns the water's plane into what looks like broken flakes, beautiful sparkles of silvery white on the surface. She stands there. Her baby's death is many months old now, and for a moment the future frightens her. It's one of those bleak distorted views, like some confusing translation.

Ice sits on her daughter's gravestone, on all the lawns of her future. Something is lost in the translation. She reflects on her last conversation with her husband and daughter, only an hour earlier:

"We'll get going now."

Grandma wants to take Sarah to see *Cinderella* in the theater.

"I'm seeing Cindela Mommy," the happy three-year-old claps, smiling.

Sherry feigns excitement for her little girl, hiding her pain for her child's sake. "Oh you're going to love it!"

He smiles. "Rest Mommy. We'll see you tonight." Her look made him add: "you need to rest." A long pause with a long look at her countenance. "I love you. We'll see you later." Her look made him worry.

Standing there at the beach recalling that earlier hour, she feels she wants this moon, in all its beauty—like glass— poured out in broken pieces over the bay, this moon to drift into a poem that might comfort her heart. It can't. Its presence poured over the water is the only thing that's beautiful.

But who will write this poem? Who will write it right, right now? God, will you? Please? My husband always wrote me poems when I was hurting. He can't now. He's hurting. His poems are part of what first won my heart. God will you write me this poem? Only you can now. Only You know what I need. The pain is impossible, she thinks, and it's been too long. She is alone.

Her husband and Sarah watch *Cinderella* in some theater up the island. But even when they are home, she feels so hellishly unattended, alone.

Sometimes the whole solar system—this planetary corner—along with all that is visible—the universe's milky way, galaxies farther—all of it is there—a close cluster of moths, butterflies, fireflies—making God seem near. Stars like sequins of gold—weightless floating—sea minnows, stones, sea glass—all lustrous, as though afloat in the deep heavens, moving in cosmic perfection, clear harmonious motion and music as heard in an English boys' choir—from God to the human heart, no distortions, no losses between, in translation. But all which brings healing and all that is good is so very far and dark. All loved ones are far. They try to move close—stumbling, self—infected sputters, fallen, broken machine fashion, so hard to run properly, speak right, act evenly, reach properly. Connections are feeble. Nothing is translated properly, accurately. Glass falls shattering with gravity, shatters as all the glass in the green house, as flakes of moonlight on the bay.

All is dark, broken. God is gone. Center Moriches is silent, insignificant. She is insignificant, tiny, invisible. This night boils with turmoil. She fears the future, the part that begins now, even before tomorrow. There's this sudden press. The moon's explosive beam seems cruel. Her daughter has been stolen. This is the night I want to die, she thinks. The invisible serpent slithers from one motionless star around another stationary star, from head to tail, millions and millions of miles everywhere above, coiling, slithering, hissing, horrid. She is alone. She walks home hauling all the weight of a sack of darkness, passing the yellow lighted squares of windows in the neighborhood, windows of homes where she imagines children don't die. This life is night; it's a slithering beast.

She has nothing against her life. It's as good, better than any or most, she rationalizes honestly, with thoughts fixed in comparative logic. Some people go through worse suffering, more loss, she understands, but it's the pain: she feels it, and for her it is unbearable. Suicide has an elastic, irresponsible exclamation. Of all the punctuation, it comes at the end of a short sentence as well. There are no phrases, clauses, no adverbs prefacing adjectives. It is to the point, and is not thought through thoroughly. Just a pressing, demanding, convenient, urgent exclamation! This is the best time. It's the most expedient way, with no parenthetical intrusions allowed. I just can't bear the pain, she thinks, convinced, forcing the eraser to smudge the guilt.

She arrives home. She finds her prescription sleeping pills, thinking there's nothing so sweet as sleep. There'll be no mean, insensitive discovery in blood. In the empty house, thinking, considering, trusting all those moon-shaped white pills to her tongue and throat to mend this one greater wound becomes a consideration she wishes she, someone, anyone can erase.

Again, my life is not as bad as so many others, she thinks. But it's the pain I can't take. I just can't take the pain. Tears, a loud shouting scream of desperation—she takes the phone off the hook. She looks at the pills in her open palm. Another scream of prayer. She imagines a book, not yet finished, closing, without a bookmark, thinks hard about swallowing away the pain; but there comes a parenthetical intruder—a still and silent, yet loud impression, a louder shout in its press than her own voice's shout within the walls, a very simple "No!"

Second thoughts emanate—Sarah, Cliff, others—reluctance to make more pain for others. It would be a succinct final sentence that brings a sudden resolution—a disappointing story, an unfinished book, she's forced to realize. She takes the handful of the bottle of pills and pours them into the toilet, flushing the luxury of a final, door closing exit.

God the master teacher teaches lessons. We learn faith, which means we expect tests. There's discipline in the faith life. This life requires endurance of faith, bravery of faith, with a result of faith, becoming triumph of faith.

We express our thanksgiving. We make our requests to God. The answer we desire doesn't arrive, and we're reminded that *"the peace of God which passes understanding"* which is precisely what's promised, comes. As one disciple asked when Jesus probed them if they would leave Him, *"Where else are we going to go? You have the words of eternal life."* We can't move away because of pain misread in our experiences. God is making us strong, stronger, strong in our weakness.

God delays often. He is a slow chess player. His "wait!" signals our answers. The great ones of the Bible were not great in their beginnings, but were made great through the lessons by processes God led them through. God fit them for their positions.

Joseph in Genesis endured insurmountable relational, emotional, and physical challenges in those chapters of his adult youth. "The word of the Lord tried him." His twenty-three—year long experience in God's classroom groomed him, had him prepared at age forty to face his family. What tested him was that word, the dream God gave him in youth—always in his heart, remembered. Those hours, questions, prison years, false accusations, separation from his loving father, stunning wounds from brothers—all contradicting the word of promise which God gave him—the promise, the dream, his hope for his future in the land of the living.

But, "when his word came", suddenly—after thirteen years of brutal, grueling waiting, he was unchained, shaven, standing before the ruler of Egypt, found ready for graduation, at age thirty commencement, the task God formed him to accomplish, to bring Himself glory—the crisis coming upon the world—foreseen, the famine foreshadowed in a dream; and then, to deal in truth and mercy in a loving, wise, and forgiving demeanor with his family, all trawled in hungry desperation to Egypt.

God speaks a promise of what He intends to accomplish; yet years pile up, pain intrudes like a beast, and the fulfillment of those promises seem remote. The first lesson to learn is that we're to expect to be taught lessons, and it's the lessons of faith building—tests, discipline, trust, courage, long suffering and more—these will bring peace and strength. The knowledge of God, and that settled acceptance of His management protect us. We allow God's rule, particularly since we once vowed, as we once prayed, "Please be my Lord and Savior."

Our hearts beat with the rhythm of seconds of a clock.

Seconds mount into minutes, hours, days… We who live on the coasts of the world see the tides rise, fall—in flawless regularity.

Seasons pass. We celebrate birthdays, count years, number our days.

Disappointments small and big become appointments. "Did I miss something?" We ask.

"Trust Me," our answer.

"Did I misinterpret You God?"

"Trust Me."

"Did the evil one trick me?" We ask after those years slide behind us, and our hair turns gray, and our energy is not what it was, and we're closer to the end.

"Trust Me, no matter what."

"Why didn't that good thing happen, that altered year occur, as I hoped, expected, believed?"

"Lean not on your own understanding. Trust Me."

"But God I'm confused."

"Know Romans 8:28, always. Trust, though I seem to slay

you. Trust, obey."

"How long Lord?"

"Not for you to know. Trust Me."

"Lord I'll trust you."

"Now you're passing the test. Now you have the victory of faith."

We count our blessings and our disappointments, which may be blessings. The prophet Habakkuk had a place with his God.

After listing the catastrophic negatives, losses, encompassing suffering, he makes his cry, "*Yet I will rejoice in the Lord; I will joy in the God of my salvation.*"

The moment after we say farewell to our earthly lives' disappointments—muddled in our temporal minds in this life—we will enter our eternal appointment with Jesus.

A year passes from this night. 1986. Cousin Maryanne is with child, expecting a boy in a few months. For good reasons she asks Sherry, "Would you be my Lamaze coach?"

This challenge brings a renewed ache to her broken wounds in loss, yet feels she should, suspecting something good may come from this. Lamaze classes, years earlier in her first pregnancy, with Cliff coaching her, return in her memory. "Okay Maryanne. I'd love to help you."

At one of the early sessions the Lamaze instructor tells her own personal stories of giving birth to a few children.

Afterward she explains that she and her husband, wanting to raise more children—without the physical birth process again—decided they would begin an adoption process into South Korea.

At the end of the session Sherry broaches: "Is there a name you could give me—the agency you're adopting through? Seems like something I may want to do."

"Of course. Is this something your husband would be in support of? That's important. Most of these agencies are big on unity, naturally."

"My husband and I have always talked about it."

"*New Beginnings Children Services*—in Mineola. Willis Avenue. Ask for our social worker Kathy Danowski. She's excellent."

"Thank you!" Thoughts overload her mind. Like color, hope is daubed to her heart. She thinks, first—the prospect; then the natural negatives—the costs—especially now. Things aren't going well at the plant—possibility of a loss of a big contract with the Air Force. Money is in question. Also, she wonders if she herself has grown immune to the stings of disappointments, or would the possibility of another defeat finish her. The fear of disappointment, like the fear of failure, is paralyzing.

She struggles with the self-examination in her soul: Do I want this for me? Or do I want it for God? Or is this for that foreign orphan who needs a home? Is it natural—these maternal instincts? Is this seed of desire in my heart planted by God?

The two years since Becky's death—and nearly three since her own close brush with death—is a dash of time still feeling too close, sorely raw. But maybe this is one of those flashes of opportunity. Maybe hearing this La Maze instructor's story is one of those divine appointments, a door cracking open, one that can't be shut; yet maybe it's the open window that could actually close. She's twenty-nine years old. Is this a now or never? Or wait and see? Should I act? Get out on a limb? Take a step of faith?

The flux of the sea is constant. The rising tide pushes forward. The toppling surf stirs sand, gravel, stones, and sea glass. The falling tide pulls backward. The sandy surface of wet shoreline is never the same, a constant flux. Sea glass seekers scour. If none walk the shore to find those pieces at any given low tide, the opportunity is lost. That rare piece of yellow-gold could be there glistening, ripe for picking—making perhaps its rare accessibility, its once in a lifetime advent, only to be plunged under, never to be seen by human eye again. Maybe taking a step—inquiring, pressing, looking—is an opportunity for that chance piece.

Soccer, a heavily defensive, low scoring, less offensive team sport presents the best philosophy for victory: to shoot at the goal at your first opportunity; don't wait or work for the best or better opportunity, as it may not come, and it may be taken from you. Strike while striking is possible.

I'll call, inquire. What can that hurt? I'll talk to my husband about it. He'll support me. She remembers that June afternoon conversation, lying recumbent with him—her husband to be, someday one day—beneath the linden tree in the arboretum.

She remembers their dialog those eleven years earlier in 1975—two kids in the huge shade lying in the late June grass—new lovers in their teens, with dreams—hers of a big family someday, of adopting abandoned ones—his willingness, his old recollections of the kind Mr. Brownlow who welcomes Oliver Twist into his home in that old Victorian story which somehow stuck with him.

VALENTINE'S DAY OWLS
Two owls
in two acmes of
tall oaks, **hoot... whoo**
One to the other—behind our place on
The frame of Haven's acreage. Forlorn,
Their blare—seamless meter, haunting lament,
ancient cause for caroling-
celebration—love's advent. One far, one near—
Back and forth nascent rhythm. Timbered symmetry—
Suggestive songs gesturing lyrics of primal love.
Two owls.

Two humans
in two nadirs of gravity—
We slink out to spy, visit to listen.
Limbs of white oaks like broken strings of violins
Sag from starry sky.

"Where are they?" we whisper,
Wish in darkness our presence won't offend.
Chorus to our author, hymn to their maker—
our whispers, their hooting.
Flashlights scour, combing shafts
through strands of branches.
Stars sparkle, dripping beams through strands of space.
We find one—a great horned—like a blessed hope
In our beam at a tree's zenith. Her heavy head ,
swivels, wide eyes stare, lower, glare down—
our haunting luster.
Moments lurch—her perch totters.
Their lilting cadence settles to silence.
Feathers ruffle. Wings lift.
She launches on silent wings.
Our light offends. Forlorn,
Two humans.

GRAFTING

When the ancient brothers Peter and Andrew heard Jesus' call, *"straightway they forsook their nets, and followed Him"* (Mark 1:18). We should be afraid to move forward without God, but when He says we should move, we should fear standing still. If we'd promptly obey that first fitting moment—neither wavering nor waiting—we could walk on water.

Adoption is God's idea—His plan since the beginning. It's what He's about. Adoption is the admittance into God's Fatherhood, His family. The Father generously adopts children, giving all the privileges as heirs. Salvation, which comes from choosing to forsake our own nets and following the eldest Son, is forgiveness, heaven, freedom from condemnation and damnation, but is also a position into a family. He escorts us in. *"...God sent forth His Son... to redeem those who were under the law, that we might receive the adoption as sons"* (Galatians 4:4,5).

The range of God's patience with mankind through the millennia is seen through adoption. We've *"received the Spirit of sonship. And by Him we cry, 'Abba (Daddy) father'"* (Romans 8:15). We're no longer slaves owned by a brutal master anymore; there's a father-child relationship now. We have a dad who's not too busy, tired, or deaf.

The full revelation of the legitimacy into our adoption, which opens through our acceptance of His invitation, is an effect fully revealed when we depart earthly life, entering His kingdom, leaving this world's corruption, becoming "like Him" in fullness. This is the inheritance promised. In antiquity believers were predestined to adoption. In the present we're assured to be heirs, sons, daughters. We are now "priests and kings" by faith. But in the future, we'll be glorified, revealed as sons and daughters of the King to all creation.

We are given a new nature and name, access to Dad (Abba), and it's provided only through the first born of all creation, the Son, Jesus, "the only begotten," who promises love, help, and more.

Social adoption of the orphaned and abandoned is a microcosm, a type, a miniature image of the God-adoption covenant. Moses was adopted by Pharaoh's daughter; Esther by Mordecai. James 1:27 postures as a premier hub in Christian living; it's placed as a self-exam in our alignment with the father's heart, stating plainly, "*Pure and undefiled religion before God and the Father is this: to assist orphans and widows in their trouble, and to keep oneself unspotted from the world.*"

The ultimate adoption is this: His death on a cross with open arms welcoming us into His family, no matter where we've been; to a place where there's plenty of room at the table. And then there's the third day in the Easter story. Often, when we think we've lost it all, He shows up.

For the next twenty years—1987 through 2007, Sherry occupies in adoptions, effectually adopting six children— each process a test of commitment, and each process respectively believed to be the last. Each of these kids' birth parents are in regretful circumstances, ominously crucial enough that they're prevented from providing care. Their offspring are put up for adoption. Each of these, plucked from the millions of abandoned ones in the world, are blessed to have birth parents who love them enough to relinquish rights—understanding they aren't capable; and love them enough—in a world of quick fix abortions—to give them life, bring to birth, and surrender them unselfishly to a better life.

Convinced there's no good thing He won't withhold from a daughter who risks taking a leap, she's discovering solid earth beneath her feet. She's held onto the assurance that her husband is as convinced as they both were, once disclosed and sorted out in their earliest days lying beneath that linden tree in the arboretum in 1975.

"The Lord is near to those who have a broken heart, and saves such as have a contrite spirit" (Psalm 34:18). Worthy things in life come out of breaking. Ground itself must be broken, plowed before planted seed can germinate into food for a world. It is the heart that's broken that pleases God. Sorrow initiates joy. *"Weeping may endure for a night, but joy comes in the morning"* (Psalm 30:5).

Marriage, the fusing union, the grafting connection of fitting parts—parts different yet suited—is intended for the duration of life of either of the parts. Marriage is one of God's means to rub out the innate selfishness in each human being. God puts us into relationships so we might get our eyes off of our isolating selves, onto another.

Jesus Christ is linked to His church in marriage. He espouses in love His bride as a chaste virgin. With this commitment He gives Himself, gives His life's blood for His bride, the church.

Jesus waits for the great day when mutual joy will be completely consummated in heaven at the marriage feast. This groom will present His bride—the church—perfect and complete—to all the universe. Until then, she waits, looking for her city, with lamps filled with burning oil for her groom to take her away. The Lord knows those who are His. His true bride is lovely and pure in character; brightly glowing in true light.

His bride wears His name, shares His wealth, shares His suffering. He hates divorce. Death won't separate Him from His bride. Jesus' engagement to His true church, for whom

He left heaven to propose, to purchase with His own blood, to promise to return for—patently becomes more than a human marriage.

He knows His true bride. The tragedy persists in that much of what the planet witnesses through what's labeled "the church" is largely a sham counterfeit, a gold-digging self-absorbed opportunist pretending to be holy and wholly given to the groom. "The Lord knows those who are His." His roster of followers is not listed on an earthly membership roster.

January 1987 begins the first leap—signing agreements, paying fees, finishing home studies—reaching into South Korea. At this time they are twenty-nine years old. The first test comes in March: the aircraft manufacturing plant is clos-ing down. The company loses Government contracts. Cliff is laid off, and this transitional limbo puts their eligibility into suspension. He returns to school for a Master's degree and that long postponed English teacher certification. Costs, time, schoolwork are suddenly piled onto erratic employment. The thought torments—what bad timing! And the big question is, should we shelve this adoption until a more "convenient" year?

Questions go to heaven. God returns with confirming verses as the two of them recurrently build confidence to con-tinue, like Psalm 60:12, *"Through God we shall do val-iantly..."* One crucial hour when she had to respond to the adoption agency the next morning, after a perplexing day of decision, Cliff is reading a bedtime book to Sarah—Dr. Suess's story about Horton the elephant. Horton is left with an egg. Mayzie is the kind of mother who gets up and leaves her egg to go on vacation.

Sarah's dismayed with this careless, selfish bird, one inter-ested more in her own pleasure in Palm Beach. Horton shows long suffering, love, persistence—all obedient willingness to anticipate bigger purposes, rather than running impetuously away, giving up. He sits on Mayzie's egg—for months, through ridicule, weather, expulsion from his home, and more, all for one little life in an egg.

This simple story unfolds in childlike newness to two adults at a critical hour of decision. Persist. Don't give up. An unexpected, uncanny way for God to answer. Are we crazy? It's flimsy, but as it relates to scriptures it compounds with, it's what we have, it's all we have—a peculiar "stay on course," directive. Wait and see.

Later in the process photos arrive—a newborn, October 3, 1987, Meong Hwa Oh, later renamed Laura Grace. By March 1988, a year after the layoff, a year of juggling dollars, it's final. Five-month old Laura arrives at Kennedy airport, placed in the arms of a happy thirty-year old mom. Her husband's new career—teaching high school English—begins this same period.

In 1989 a posting from the agency welcomes applicants for children. In South Korea many babies are waiting. Tugged again, Sherry applies, is accepted, which to her becomes the "go ahead" divine direction. They walk through another home study, and follow up with a building addition—second story, doubling the size of the Center Moriches house.

Photographs of Eun Hyuk later renamed Thomas Nathan, born December 14, 1990 arrive. Construction begins on the house December 26, is complete in February—plenty of room and time for Tom's May arrival. Sherry's finished with the size of her family; at least she supposes.

In 1993 she inclines to explore grafting another in—when a timely call from Kathy Danowski rings with news of an abundance of needy South Korean babies. The obstacle?

There's simply no more money. Flight fees, agency fees, legal fees, medical fees after the two seem insurmountable a third time. Impossible—even the initial $600.00 application fee at that time exceeded their funds. "Okay God, give us enough, over our living expenses, for step one of another process, if this is your plan."

Later that week, one spring morning when a decision is needed to be reached—of all possible sources, one of Cliff's students seeks out his eleventh grade English teacher, "Mr. Schrage! Mr. Schrage!"

"Tad?"

With a bold grin: "I'm supposed to give this to you—for your family. I know it. God told me to give you this. I don't give my money to rich churches. It's a waste." Tad holds out a roll with $600.00 in cash. "God told you?"

"Yes."

"Tad this is unheard of. I can't take this from you. It doesn't feel right. What would your parents say? You worked for this. You're my student for Cryin' out loud. This is humbling to say the least. But let me tell you what's going on— right now—this week. You're not going to believe this."

Tad is a very humble, unostentatious kid with a fantastic sense of humor.

(Incidentally, twenty years later an adult Tad Agoglia was documented in a television special as a CNN Top Ten Hero of the year for his unobtrusive volunteerism with his *First Response Team of America* through his excavation and crane company.

He was chosen in 2015 by the *RUMI Forum* of Washington, DC to receive the RUMI *Peace and Dialogue Award for Extraordinary Commitment of Service*. He won the *Jefferson Award* for public service, has been featured in MSNBC, PBS, USA Today, Good Morning America, The Wall Street Journal, People Magazine's *Heroes Among Us*, among other outlets and awards.)

This small spark ignites the next adoption. Photos of Chan Ho, later renamed Zachary James, arrive. Born May 23, 1994, Zachary's process moves slowly, with glitches, hold-ups, multiple confusions in the administration process that nearly thwart its completion. In February 1995 he finally arrives at

nine months old. Four children and one in heaven make five.
They're done. Their nest is full, they suppose.

Mom and Dad—Nancy and Pat—move to Hamden,
upstate New York in the Catskill Mountains, and Sherry and
Cliff on a visit one evening sit on their rustic porch while the
kids are in bed. It's Labor Day weekend. This bucolic setting
shows signs of bursts of autumn: goldenrod, cooler nights,
tints of orange in sugar maples—signs of change emerging.
Sherry recognizes the coming years in this tranquil place as a
sort of last stop on the train of life for her parents. She's pensive, hearing the subdued sound of crickets. With all the
adjustments tied with kids this time of year, school is beginning this coming week.

"What's up. You're quiet."

"Everything," she says. Crickets peep in the still gloom.

"What do you mean?"

"Time goes too fast."

"It does."

"Sarah's already fourteen."

"Hard to believe."

"Laura's nine."

"I know. Tom's six. Zak's three."

"I feel sad," she says—a tone of frustration.

He waits a moment. "How do you mean?"

A tear on her face. She brushes it away. "Just disappointed. It all keeps haunting me. I'm almost forty."

"Me too. I'm ahead of you. I got ten days left for me." A
laugh.

"I still feel frustrated with family."

"How? Why?"

"You know"—a tone of impatience.

Silence.

"Help me."

"You know what I mean. People don't see adopted children as your own. Even family. They say stupid things like, 'Sarah's your own child.' They don't see adopted kids right. They don't get it."

"You see them as our own."

"I know."

"I do too."

She nods, wiping eyes.

"But it really isn't important, to me—what anyone says or thinks." A long pause.

He adjusts his posture in the wicker chair. "Not all people. But I guess we expected that. We were told that, about even family—to expect that. People just talk before they think. You're right, they don't get it. I just don't even care what anybody thinks or says. I don't think it's intentional."

"I know, I do though. I guess I shouldn't care, but I do."

"About?"

"Care what people think."

"God is aboard though. That gives me a little peace. I'm okay with everything. Not as disappointed like you I guess."

A breeze blows warmly. The leaves whisper. They sit quietly for minutes.

"Summer's over. Can't believe school starts Wednesday. I don't feel ready."

She quietly feels the frustration.

"I'm not ready. Never feel like I am. Not happy about going back in the classroom, that's for sure."

She broods quietly, can't help but believe he doesn't care, is insensitive, preoccupied. Everyone is insensitive, she thinks, except maybe other women in my circumstance.

"Sherry I wish I could change things. I wish I could make all our pain and sorrow go away. I wish I could fix it all—Rebekah—everything, but I can't. I'm sorry."

"See that's just it. You want to fix everything. I know you

can't. I just want you to *listen*! I just need someone to listen, to understand, to try to understand."

"I'm listening. I'm here!"

She sobs, rises, enters her parents' new home. He hears her steps ascend the stairs. She stills her sobs—her kids sleeping.

She completely reckons her adopted ones are no less "her own" kids, but people see differently, she imagines, as she wishes she didn't care what any people thought. Insensitive ones make ignorant comments. She wishes it were like water beading on glass; but it's not. It seeps into her heart, stays there, and the despair feels so much like anger.

The next day they don't talk. There's a long private examination of her own thoughts, beliefs, emotions, an awkwardness between each—a resentment. He doesn't want to fumble the ball, doesn't want to carry the ball either. She won't talk because she believes he's too consumed with other cares. Even her own husband doesn't get it.

When school begins, feelings and imaginations are once again remedially drowned out by the hectic business of busy September life.

It's 1997.

"But we can't afford it. Never mind raising another—that alone is taxing. The costs are astronomical now. Fifteen to twenty thousand now?"

"Domestic adoption. Kids here need homes too."

"But that costs too."

"No. No, not always."

Little Flower Children's Services in Brooklyn promotes a Foster-to-Adopt program. Kids are abandoned, orphaned, or removed from bad situations.

She takes a step forward to inquire. Soon they both enroll in a required course.

Months pass. Diana Miller, later renamed Abigail Faith,

born February 7, 1998 arrives one week later—a newborn. She arrives like a little doll with a full head of dark hair. Her birth mother asserts she herself is Cherokee, not knowing who the father is.

It's this uncertainty, an anticipation of trouble with a birth parent's potential change of mind, with the whole foster-to—adopt process, that's disconcerting. Having the hope for adoption without permanent guarantee, with the heartache of relinquishing after bonding, makes Sherry reluctant, bracing against a broken heart. Only months before Abby's arrival she has to relinquish Darnel, a boy. His aunt—sister of his unstable birth mom—stepped in with the court's rights after a month's hesitation, suddenly removing the child from Sherry's unsuspecting arms.

It's the system—the courts' clumsy, sometimes erroneous attempt at balancing between what's in a child's best interest and what rights a negligent or abusive parent has—that creates a problem, provoking a duel over custody, a dual priority system. Sometimes a remiss parent becomes the client, rather than the child. Allowing time for perhaps any given drug addicted parent to get his or her act together, while the child languishes in the system, often at length and uncertainty, sometimes cared for by several, is what often turns out bad.

While Abby is secure in their custody, her troubled birth mother does decide to step in demanding custody. Regular visits ensue in frequency until it's settled. She accesses free legal aid despite abandoning her daughter, and the record of negligence on her older child. She begins her case, throwing the Schrages into a three year legal battle, with weekly trips to Brooklyn, costs, loss of time at work, a lawyer, and more. Attached with affection to Abby, there is no thought of turning back.

There's reasons Abby was removed from her birth mother. I can't believe this. She herself should have been adopted when she was born. Her parents hurt her. It's sad, and I know she wants Abby, but she can't have her. No way.

Not now.

The court battle is draining. Finally, after three consecutive court appointments are ignored by Abby's birth mom, the judge decides—finally—that her rights are to be terminated. She seems to have disappeared.

***

2002. During these adoption years, on vacation at Prince Edward Island with the kids, with an idea of buying a piece of property, they tour with open eyes. On a sunny day on the island's east end, on Panmure Island a real estate sign–a two story house built on a sublime rise on a field with water view. "That's the house I had a dream of. Oh God. It's for sale!" Sherry says.

Before the vacation even ends, finances, documents, and signatures are in order. The contract's set for closing in September. A summer house, a Christmas and Easter sanctuary. She's thrilled.

Panmure Island is a four-mile round haven, heaven's best glimpse on this planet. Lavender, plum, purple lupine; a hundred June greens; red cliffs, earth, shore; a lot of sea; so much sky.

God's road map reveals these sanctuaries in sojourns in the journey, always with His rest. It's a bumpy, sometimes treacherous journey, with an itinerary including bereavements, contests, engagements, medical threats, raising kids, sadness, confusion, financial paralysis, yet always with proofs of His presence, guidance, restful sanctuary.

The equilibrium of God's peace is detected. Sadness and confusion surfaces with life's events, both threatening with weakening mental depression—the kind King David dueled with, speaking to himself in his forty-second Psalm, *"Why are you cast down, O my soul? And why are you disquieted within me? Hope in God; For I shall yet praise Him, the help of my countenance and my God,"* and in other Psalms. The famous king learned to seek assistance in his flaws and in the numerous tunnels of dark discouragement God allowed him to travel through.

One tranquil summer morning Cliff and the boys take the sixteen-foot open boat fishing from Panmure to Boughton Island, five miles into the Gulf of St. Lawrence. Daring? Not on a calm day. But in an unforetold turn of an hour, with suddenness, wind raises waves that fold into white caps. The return to Panmure Island takes over an hour, averting two capsizing close calls. Tom and Zak find it all exciting.

Jesus sent his twelve across Galilee to the other side while He Himself stayed back to pray. In dark hours a perfect storm, cries of desperation, a contest with death, a vision of a "ghost" turning out to be Jesus Himself walking over waves—all surprise them with paralyzing fear. Lessons about realities and real peace are only found through experiencing storms, crises. Jesus calms storms—on oceans and in emotions.

Fear? Discouragement? Grief? Confusion? Hopelessness? All real, yet anyone can find joy's reason by looking upward, preparing with the great apostle who was told beforehand, "how much he will suffer for My sake," in bearing His name to this world. We can *"be of good cheer… not afraid,"* certain He is with us in our storms. Peter's request: *"Lord, if it is you, command me to come to you on the water."*

" 'Come!' and when Peter had come down out of the boat, he walked on the water toward Jesus "

The metaphor allied with Peter's literal walk expresses its clout in wide-ranging facets. Peter's step of faith reveals the grafting—the red and yellow, zeal and wisdom. Step out of a boat in a storm? Wise? If Jesus calls, and only when He calls, it is wisdom, as crazy as the natural eye sees it, yet it is wise. The remaining followers remain in the "safety" of the boat.

Also, the apostle Paul was held under arrest aboard a cargo-passenger ship in a violent storm headed for Rome. The wet, weeks' long mayhem threatened over two hundred lives. *"Take heart… I believe God that it will be just as it was told me,"* (Acts 27) he assured all, having been visited by an angel. God often works in the most mysterious ways.

Adopt six, Sherry, with modest income and health problems?

Laughable. Attempt to graft into your complicated life more complicated lives from problematical situations? Foolish, unless the Master orchardist with the arborist's tool, working in the grove of the world does the grafting. Listen. Hear God's voice, call? Get out of the boat.

***

Orange is a graft of two primary colors. Orange sea glass is the rarest. One out of ten thousand pieces is found in true orange. Unlike yellow its origin is earlier, from the turn of the twentieth century; but like it, from a certain dinnerware, a noted seldom produced brand name of glassware. In the sea glass collectors' scope, this is common knowledge: of all the low tides, finding an ample piece in orange would heighten a serious sea glass searcher's year. It will probably never come.

The color orange has come to evince the western symbol of the sun and fire, endurance and strength. It's the blend, as said, of the passion and zeal of red and the prudence of yellow. It is temperance, the grafted combination of two merging meters of color, creating new color, new life.

Through these decades, hepatitis C—contracted through those 1984 post birth transfusions—has taken its slow deteriorating strokes on Sherry's liver. She lives through two unsuccessful, one-year-long treatment journeys of interferon—three shots a week—each cycle spaced with a one-year buffer between, each increasing with hopefulness as the drug increases effectiveness through improvements. The treatments produce dreadful side effects—uncomfortable at best, agonizing at worst. The prospect of a liver transplant emerges with strong consideration and looming urgency. This latest hepatitis virus has become another silent killer. God, where are you?

In 2004 after the last fifty week treatment, the liver specialist decides to continue radically prescribing injections for twelve more months. This time the drug *ribavirin* is added, which depletes red blood cells; so shots of *procrit* have to be added to balance that problem. After twelve months there's no change.

The doctor suggests that adding six more months in some cases have turned things around. They move forward for another harrowing six months.

The last injection of this six month run lands on Easter Sunday that year, and she hopes it's a sign—always desperate for a sign.

A visit with the specialist. Normally stoic, he's happy. These last treatments prove to be the panacea—the means of final triumph after a painfully daunting war. She's cured. Her liver has begun to restore. Persistence seems to have opened the door for God's healing. God has certainly used medicine and physicians for healing.

It's in the midst of this physical battle and custody battle over Abby, the *Little Flower* social worker brings to Sherry's attention a baby boy. Another adoption? She knows it seems fanatical, yet wants to, discerning puzzlingly that she's supposed to, but is pessimistic about her husband's willingness. She decides that his unwillingness, if it yielded—unimaginably—without any persuading, would attest it to be God's prompting again—a kind of answer—as in Gideon's fleece of wool—despite the challenges in their lives, despite the circumstantial appearances of their recent episodes. She prays, prepares, deciding that afternoon how to tell him about Raymond Vasquez, who would later be renamed Gabriel Joseph, born April 29, 1999.

Her husband returns from another weekday of work, announcing as he barges into the back door, even before Sherry's proposition—"I think God spoke to me on the drive home."

"What? What about?"

"Sounds crazy. I don't get it—probably bad timing, but—can't believe I'm saying this—but we're supposed to adopt again. Am I crazy?"

"Oh my God. You're not going to believe this…" She apprises of Gabriel's situation, the social worker's call that very afternoon.

Gabe is born into a Latino family with six siblings—half brothers and half sisters—all crammed into their seventy-five-year-old grandmother's tiny Bronx apartment.

By 2004 both adoptions are complete, satisfying the New York City courts, warranting a catered celebration. Abby and Gabe's addition means Sherry's the mother of seven, not excluding Rebekah.

It's in 2005, Pat and Nancy now living in Hamden, New York in the Catskill Mountains face their worst crisis. Nancy has battled, and now acceded to bone cancer. With help of hospice, her last week in the spring of 2005 brings Sherry, Gary, and Robbie to her bedside.

In and out of consciousness, her closing days are accented, drowned in her voice's intermittent cries, "Daddy! Daddy! Why Daddy? Why?"

For days she cries this in a semi-conscious state, returning in her mind to that occasion of her own childhood when her dad's abandonment of the family damaged her brothers, mother, herself—his only daughter. Now knocking on the door of heaven, a sixty-seven-year-old becomes a hurt ten-year-old again, wrestling with a half century old ache, a long-standing, deep-rooted issue before her departure. It's a long leap back, never having voiced a word about it in her adult-hood, scarcely even alluded to that trauma in childhood, until now. With some help with understanding from Uncle Paul—of that disconnect back then, Sherry is apprised of how gravely that abandonment affected her mom as a child, giving her, Rob, and Gary a hint—perhaps—into why their mom sometimes seemed insensitive, even cold and indifferent at phases through their lives. As she passes they see their mom differently—now retrogressed—a little hurt girl in a grown woman's failing frame.

In 2006, browsing websites online into the newly opened adoption doors into Ethiopia, with no serious intention of adding to her family, she runs into a picture of a certain three—year old boy—Elshaday who would later be renamed Samuel Elshaday. The light turns on again. In the spring of 2007, having mustered up $20,000.00 for this foreign adoption cost, the two of them fly for a ten-day legal exchange orientation, settling Sam's adoption. They escort him—at age five—home to New York to be their youngest, last, eighth child. Sherry will turn fifty in 2007.

An interesting phenomenon occurs. Sam shared a bed in the Ethiopian orphanage, in Addis Ababa, with another boy, Mookie, who is also being adopted at this time. This timing for the two of them is impeccable in that it averts any possible sadness for either, if one of them were left behind. Most of the numerous Ethiopian children are not as fortunate to find a family, making this unusual. The further a child advances from infancy, anywhere in the world, statistically, the less likely he'll have opportunity to be grafted into a home. An older child is simply not as adoptable.

Above this "coincidence," it is divulged through the agency that, of all the possible places in the western world an African child might be sent, Mookie is also becoming adopted, coming to Long Island, New York. He'll reside a mere twenty-five miles away.

Above this coincidence—Long Island being replete with over four million residents—Mookie is being adopted by Mike and Patricia Cisek. Mike was a high school friend of Sherry and Cliff thirty-three years earlier. This timeliest miracle continues and reignites relationships. Some happenstances can't help but shout, "God's design!" Two needles in three haystacks? Hardly coincidence. There is a God who through workings like this reveals His intimate acquaintance with every human's experience.

Jeremiah 33:3: *"Call to Me, and I will answer, and show you great and mighty things."*

IN WHITE RIVER JUNCTION
The Connecticut cuts into the White, two rivers
Converge in a merging graft into one,
parting Vermont from New Hampshire
where interstates transect, rails intersect,
and light stands in irremediable noon,
meeting ground between green peaks.

Luminous moon kindles
this union of moving rivers to silver fire.
Dawn's lower pasture lures hybrid bovines—
Scores of cross breeds across orchard's border.
Morphology and fog hold morning
In level rows of even trees.

Daylight rises. Mooing baritones lift mist to sun.
The knife of the arborist grafts new life—
Fruit mixtures, textures, living tissue in fitting v's.
Between green hills in White River Junction—
This splicing of rails, rivers, roads;
This fusing of day and night; this grafting of boughs—

We sort through our lives in a grade crossing,
through our mounded memories
in our growing old, as though into
the valley of a duvet hands hold at corners.
Trains leave, bovines breathe deep cellos,
Knives cut lives, graft lives.

The sounds of rivers' whispers—
Their sea bound waters shift, flow, float
Like sails on a sea of air. Highways' sighing hisses,

falling limbs, train whistles, cows at rest—all meld.
We move away from tomorrows
in White River Junction.

RED REFLECTIONS

On a summer midnight sitting on the deck looking upward at the milky way, she imagines God's ability to see her in her smallness, there in a reclined chair on Panmure Island, Prince Edward Island. I'm a speck, she thinks, on a tiny island off a bigger island, in Canada, on the North American continent, this hemisphere, planet earth. He sees from beyond the milky way, beyond the universe's end—if there is such an end. She ponders the idea that "*men should seek the Lord, in the hope that they might grope for him and find Him, though He is not far from each one of us; for in Him we live and move and have our being.*" (Acts 17:27,28) She wonders at His omnipresence, His habitation within her.

"God show me a shooting star." An hour passes. Mosquitos' drones raid her ears, pricking skin at those curves the repellent missed. Time to go in.

The incredulous thinker, the audacious atheist speaking before his audience—"God if you're there I dare you in the next five minutes to strike me dead. You don't exist. If you do, you can't be a God of love with all that happens around this planet. I dare you. You can't, you won't—because you aren't real. It will never happen."

To think we can exhaust the patience of God in five minutes, and to dare to test him with shooting star fleeces are two human misunderstandings. Humans, so prone to faithlessness, lean upon natural senses.

To imagine God not as a God of love because of harm that happens around this planet is to ignore the blatant brevity of life, man's free will, and all that He's done to rescue us, secure us, and usher us into an eternity where real life begins. He's paid a debt he didn't owe, one no one could pay. He pardons, with His offer: "You don't owe a thing!" Just trust Me, put faith in My Son and the death He died, the resurrection He authenticated, the price He paid."

God has rationale in every "No" in life. People dread, even panic regarding prayer "not being answered," while a wise divine Father always answers, synthesizing responses to supplications often in collective and far fuller ways than we anticipate. Faith waits in patience, expects explanation, which may not arrive until the revelation promised in the end. God has never taken anything from anyone without giving more. David inquired in Psalm 39, "*Lord, what do I wait for? My hope is in You.*" And Job in his first chapter, "*The Lord gave… and has taken away.*" When we belong to Him, He's willing and able to give a hundred after He takes one; and He's right and just to take a hundred, if He so wills.

Psalm 46:1 announces, "*God is… help in trouble.*" And we ask, "Why didn't God help me earlier?"

First He fits us to the trouble, molding us. His vow: "*I will be with Him in trouble; I will deliver him and honor him.*" He is with us in our trouble, and then frees us from it in His good season. Again, He trusts us with the tribulation he allows us to bear. "You can do this," He assures. We can wish and pray our trial away, or we can view the trial as an opportunity to watch Him work out something valuable through the ordeal. One promise is well-defined, "*…in Me you may have peace. In the world you will have tribulation; but be of good cheer, I have overcome the world*" (John 16:33).

Human experience sometimes makes little sense, seems to arrive from an insensitive empty source. Life's trials can crash upon us like Atlantic breakers. They smack, knock, tumble, throw us—as though with a persona saying, "I don't care, and there's no God that cares."

Often God seems not to make sense, even to some with Biblical sense; and of course people often make no sense. The Christian experience is inundated with what seems to be senselessness.

Solomon, the wisest that ever lived in ancient years, said that there were too many books in his day. (Ecclesiastes 12). That was five thousand years ago. "*Let us hear the conclusion of the whole matter,*" he said. "*Fear God and keep His commandments, for this is the whole duty of man. For God will bring every work into judgment, including every secret thing, whether it is good or whether it is evil.*" There's an awful lot of irony in his "wisdom"—as he clung to a thousand women who led him astray in the last years his life (1 Kings 11). Solomon sadly shrank away from his allegiance to God. That seems senseless.

With so many books, of which even titles of some are long complex sentences, we grow confused. We wander through decades down corridors of bookstores, Amazon.com, libraries… ramblings in print (like these you're reading) written by some which are scarcely sane, scratching our heads striving to make sense of all that's perplexing in life. We're beggars sharing the little we have. The ironies in the human race are more recurrent than commonsense. We feel the need to be heard, to have something to say, stories worth telling. Write, sing, shout, design, speak, recite, paint, dance, act, perform—there's a record—breaking clamor of cries and public statements in rivalry to be heard, understood, seen, felt. Hands reach high, voices crying, "Pick me! Pick me!"

Sherry sends money to a "non-profit" relief organization, only to discover later its president earns a whopping half a million as an annual salary. Non-profit? That's the end of that. Senseless. "It's wrong," she says.

Some folks live in excess, some with little. "Take only what you need, not too much!"

Years of membership in their Long Island mega church,

serving on boards, committees, outreaches, have the both of them scrutinizing, reluctantly brought to close view to the accounting details of what functions more like an American corporation than the church of God, that in no way models a prescription of the earliest church in New Testament history.

The world's abundant collections of art, too many books, music… too much luggage, too much stuff—storage facilities besides sizable homes—capacitated, containers, financial accounts, people building "bigger barns," like manna stored, spoiling moldy and stale. There's a lot of irrational hoarding in a transient world.

It's poor thought and impetuous impulse that makes us falter.

A televised professional soccer player falls to his knees, leans forward, landing on his chest in a defensive diving header, sending the airborne ball to safety out of bounds. "Use your foot!" a living room fan shouts. Two interior home construction workers work toward their goal—the tall one on his knees building baseboards, the short one on a ladder refining ceiling molding. Examples are endless.

We grow into old age, accumulate mounds of time working in mundaneness, mounting wealth or dying broke. In retrospect we quote in paraphrases, "Vanity of vanities," then resort to talking to God more in the course of finishing what's left in our journeys, justifying what we believe He has assigned—no matter how ostensibly meaningless the past, present, future may look to us.

Like new glass the present-day reveals all details in translucence. Then time like the sea shatters it into fragments, obscures it like fog; and the further in time, the purer, softer, more visually muddled, allowing only light through. We see through the less transparent through our memory, rummaging through the murkiness of the past—which in time surfaces as distorted and surreal as a dream which gradually fades after waking.

At the house in Canada, Cliff has to replace a serpentine belt on the deck of the riding mower one July morning: pulleys, bolts, adjustments needing proper tools, intricacies not so simple for one with only pliers and a screw driver, undersupplied in mechanical temperament fifteen miles from town. Spellbound with engineering complexity, he finds himself talking to an absent designer, asking why he didn't invent soundly, putting a bolt there, or building a guard here, beginning to understand the mechanism. He knows he'll never write to the company, predicting no one will read.

Planes crash, cars are recalled, engineers die, pens dry, art is stolen, investors unnerve… he muses to himself, working with parts strewn on his dew-covered overgrown lawn.

The repair is finished. Mow later. Eat breakfast. The kids ride ahead on bikes to the beach. He and Sherry will follow. The barn, with two glass windows and an open door, invites a blue jay inside. Removing the bikes, he finds the creature fluttering above, struggling in the heights before the shielding window of inviting light, flapping against it, trying to exit, misconstruing this strange, deceptive, man-made glass. He grips a long furring strip to nudge and steer the animal to fly to the lower open door. The frantic bird moves away. Its wings jet itself in fright into the farther high pane on the opposite side of the barn, rather than the open door, and it crashes, sending itself to the floor. The bird is breathing, panting through open beak, one eye closed, one open, disoriented, unable to return to flight. Its nearness as it lay on a dirty floor away from its natural screeching perch and flight, appears bizarre, wrong.

He takes its form in his palms. Her wings seem immobile. He carries it out onto the lawn. Sherry watches, "Oh no. Poor bird, what happened?"

"Flew into the glass window inside."

"Silly bird—what did you do to yourself? We have to keep this door shut so they don't fly in."

"Or open those windows."

"I'll get water."

"Don't know if he's thirsty."

She returns with a jar cap filled with water, balancing, avoiding spills. She places it by its beak. "Maybe she got a concussion or something. She'll come to."

They watch, wait. There's no interest in water.

"What our world does to these creatures. Poor bird." She only watches.

"What do birds know about glass. All they know is light and space. It's like we set them up for harm. What a crazy world." She exhales.

"A man driving at night hits a doe. It's dead, but he realizes an unborn fawn is in its womb, alive."

"Oh that's awful."

"He doesn't know what to do. The doe is already stiff. He rolls it into the canyon. Happens beside a canyon."

"Oh how sad."

"I always think of that poem.'*Traveling through the Dark*,' William Stafford."

"Oh I thought it really happened. It's just a poem."

"It happened—at least he says it happened."

"Aw."

"Well that's the extent of that short poem—four quatrains and a couplet."

In minutes this bird regains some exertion, moving, cricking, crawling, then raising its wings, advancing inches on the earth's green floor, absent from its sky. Unable to fly, somehow instinctually it moves its frame into the edge of the woods, yards away—like a fresh-caught trout flapping toward its river.

Questions cross Sherry's mind—anatomical ones—a bird's spine, brain—brain damage? Does it have a nest with babies? How long does a blue jay live?

"Let's catch up with the kids. Maybe it will fly again.

We'll look when we come back."

"Maybe a fox will find it."

"Maybe a coyote."

"Stop," she says. "Sad."

They pedal to the beach. Kids swim, fly a kite, balance on skim boards, shovel in wet sand. She takes her walk, finds sea glass. They return up the hill for lunch and mowing grass, and they probe the woods without finding the bird.

"I hope it flew away."

"I think it did."

Glass windows, like fences, are made to contain and keep elements out. Some panes are made to keep things out, and some are made to keep things in, or both, but it's mostly about light.

As August Wilson says through his character Bono in the climax of his play *Fences*, "Some people build fences to keep people out and other people build fences to keep people in." Walls, fences, windows, locks, doors, boundaries, barriers.... all necessities, consequences, proofs of the fall of man, originating from the very beginning after the fall in the garden, then east of Eden, extending even into heaven around New Jerusalem which boasts *"a great and high wall with twelve gates, and twelve angels at each of the gates"* (Revelation 21:12).

BOX TURTLE
Her shell's hard wary camouflage
full of greenish russet, ruby, pumpkin tints.
Her lower plate holds leathery yellow
Like the foot sole of a primordial warrior.
Her neck stretches, always on a threshold of
bashful retraction. She's like an army tank.
Claws dig, legs push... press in essence of mission,
expression of meekness, tedious crawling motion,
groveling serious slowness, purpose—
eggs, water, food...

Her rare arrival scarcely flashes.
Her soft-life's refinement lights with life.
We chance in happenstance.
She appears in wildflowers, weeds.
Child-like we realize she's not common stone.
Sudden surprise plunks wonder in our eyes.
These creatures live a hundred years.

All those decades ago—spacious pieces of past—
Rooms full of human time
form in shapes of these turtle shells—
vaults filled with stages, phases in hopes,
like coins, jewels, gold in drawers of vaults—
stock piles—charms of time
hiding in slow crawling persistence toward destinations—
moving always slowly forward toward some
forthcoming future—claws, legs, pressing, pushing...
pieces of time, increased dividends,
securities for a hope chest,
saved pieces, saved peace... "tomorrow and tomorrow..."
We shrink our valor in caves of fear,
Cover in safety as we hear
False alarms, traces of risk, rumbles, roaring motors,
Frights in familiar fancy.

After summer weeks without rain
Dark clouds spread west—ominous
Flashes, thunders—at last the deluge.
Gutters fill. Puddles pool in recessed grass
Earth is hard, impeding seepage.
The surge rests; sun bursts.

Our legs push... press in essence of mission.
We walk a wet trail, reach the bridge across the creek,
come to our seventh decade.
Just ahead headstones stand like sentinels.
We stop, waver. We stroll, slower.

I'm mowing. Mundane daydreaming—then, surprise—
My blade hits one of these reptiles.
She was unseen, hidden, until I saw too late—
legs, head—all of her a

withdrawn introversion—remote, solitary—
held in her shell of secrecy, her ward of mystery
deceptive sense of safety inside a case of darkness
Upon her lower, leathery, yellowed plate bottom.

This engine driven blade severs her swiftly in two.
Bits of shell, greenish russet, ruby, pumpkin tints in
Blemished splashes—wet red in summer cuttings.
I close the mower's roar,
sit amid this slaughter, cover closed eyes, face, forehead
in open palms in summer hush. I hope she was old,.
muse gloomily over our world,
this tilted, fallen sphere—waiting, ruminating…
These creatures live a hundred years.

In time I turn.
I uncover the shovel, dig a shell shaped hole,
scraping the entrails, burying remains—
this curtailed life—a turtle's verve;
then I pull the cord. The engine roars.
I continue this mundane mowing.

God's creatures get lost. They get hurt, become confused, and they get killed. It's a fallen world. Sometimes they don't know they're lost. Sometimes too late they learn that they're in a dangerous place. This happens to God's other precious creatures too, people.

And it is when Sherry's forty-nine, and her brother Gary is forty-eight, a man with a family, a man in trouble—on leave from his service as a policeman, with severe PTSD, having worked dedicatedly for years in the busiest precinct in the world, in Brooklyn, New York, having seen and experienced untold horrors and misery.

His contact with Sherry is regular. He welcomes her prayers, in a place of danger where because of his marital conflict and threat to himself, he is forbidden to see his children- the two younger ones still in their teens. In these months Sherry and Gary are once again close, as they were in childhood, a tightened bond of love and commiseration.

Sherry, being the oldest sibling, has taken on that sense of responsibility that supersedes blame and liability. Her thought: if not me, then who?

She is Holden Caulfield in *The Catcher in the Rye*, who, moving toward the novel's resolution, united with his sister Phoebe, says, "…nobody's around, nobody big--I mean, except me. And I'm standing on the edge of some crazy cliff. What I have to do, I have to *catch* them. That's all I'd do all day. I'd just be the catcher in the rye and all. I know it's crazy…" Sherry feels that nervous responsible sense of love and commitment.

Shakespeare in *Hamlet* says through Claudius, "When sorrows come, they come not single spies but in battalions," after multiplying tragedies in the play, meaning, "When it rains, it pours." Sometimes in life, this seems true.

Sherry's last words with her brother are spoken on Sunday, a few days before February 13, 2008. They are works coupled with scripture verses, prayers, and encouragement.

"I can't make it tonight for dinner Sher."

"Oh, Gary. We were looking forward to you coming. The kids were hoping."

"Nah I just can't." He's choking back tears.

"It will do you good."

A long silence.

"Gary?"

"Just too depressed Sher. Sorry."

Sherry thinks. She will say what she's said a dozen times to her little brother, in yet a new paraphrase: "Gary, things will change. They always do. You'll get to see Kimmy and Chris again. Yes, it's been rainy for you for a long while, but skies will clear. They always do. A lot of people are praying for you, Gary. You are so loved…"

Their conversation ends. He promises to take a raincheck. "I'll come over when I get back from visiting Dad."

Pop urged Gary to come upstate to Hamden where he still

lived, where he still grieved the loss of his Nancy who passed away twenty months earlier, and where Gary, Sherry, and Rob said their last good-byes.

On Wednesday evening February 13th, Uncle Bob calls with the news that Gary took his own life.

Finding a way after the suicide of a loved one is unexplainably difficult. The ones left behind have to make a journey that is impossibly painful. The intensity of the issues of the survivors is heartbreaking. The dark emotions blossom overhead hurriedly, one after another—as clouds or waves in a storm at sea: fear, anger, apathy, depression, confusion, numbness, shock, disbelief, stages of grief, guilt…. are endless, intense, rapid, rabid.

I should have seen this coming. If only I'd called him more often. I'm afraid of preserving my other relationships now but I need them more now. I'm desperate. This will never go away. I failed him. If only…. I could have done more, said something more, done and said differently. Healing will never come. Guilt will never cease its haunting.

Sherry connects with a grief support group, which "little by little" helps overcome what seems impossible.

T.S. Eliot wrote, "Humankind cannot bear very much reality," which Sherry learns applies to the one who falls to suicide, and the ones then left in its wake. The moments of truth come to her— make or break moments: I will never see Gary again in this life. Real Christians do commit suicide. People suffering from the atrocious realities they witness and experience, succumbing to the pain that surfaces from them, often expire in this manner. The pain is just too painful, and a merciless judgment has no place here. Gary and the ones left behind are the blue jays caught in the windowed barn, the box turtle crawling across the lawn before the mower. God's creatures get lost.

Sibling bonds are often taken for granted. Sherry has lost an ally, and in some ways, a best friend. Gary has been a protector. "My little brother is gone," is an offense that recreates her many memories with Gary into ones especially poignant, and clearly focused.

The family has changed. A key ingredient in the chemistry of family is gone. We're left behind. Where are you, God? Where were you? Things are too different now. God help me survive. God open a door of hope.

***

Panmure Island, Prince Edward Island—summers stretch across these twenty years since the turn of the millennium.

July and August weeks are filled with reading, bonfires, writing, walking, cycling, sea glass searches, entertaining, church, boating, fishing, seal watching, painting, building, reflecting, labor and rest; and they scroll by quickly.

Within this 2010-2016 lapse, accompanied with Abby, Sherry joins up with *Buckner International*, a global outreach to orphans—in ten-day mission trips to Guatemala, Belize, and Honduras. Medical help, provisions, especially new shoes for kids who have none, and Bible lessons fill the time.

The ongoing program, *Shoes for Orphan Soles* is far reaching.

On one trip, "This has never happened," says the program director. Abby, with her mom in Honduras, is recognized by a young male orphan, from a year-old photo placed with shoes Sherry shipped into the third world. Any country could receive any box of shoes—Haiti, Cambodia, Zimbabwe, Peru... The shoes go to whomever might receive—one of hundreds of thousands of boxes in a two year time frame to thirty-two possible countries, on a chance afternoon, out of five orphanages visited, this went to Honduras for one to receive, converging with Sherry and Abby. Are three needles in three haystacks found by coincidence? For this young man to recognize Abby in a photo taken with four of her brothers a year earlier, and for the package—shoes, note, and photo—to come into the young man Aaron's possession that afternoon, all crossing paths, is miraculous—what are the odds? The pair of shoes was shipped a year earlier. An article is published in *God Stories*, Buckner missions magazine at the time, highlighting specifics in this anomaly. God has a way of showing us His intimate involvement in all our lives.

Sherry also enters missions into bringing support to women in Belize struggling with circumstances in marriages, families, society. She teaches lessons learned through her own trials, losses, and gains, bringing the story of Christ's blood shed redemption. These trips to Central America seize many of her energies through these years.

***

The most coveted, hard-won color to find in the sea glass quest is red. Red stands out. Many of these pieces derive from broken reflector light lenses. In the states, red glass was not mass produced because of the colorants' costs necessary for pigment. The metal additive for the color is gold—one reason red sea glass is rare. The common knowledge in the sea glass society says it comes from these car, boat, and other vehicle light lenses made from glass, made earlier than the 1940's, before the plastic invasion. Many come from nautical signal lanterns and buoy indicators which for an enduring interval of history helped ships in navigation.

Most are tumbled by the surf long enough to make smooth—making the pieces tough to discern their origin. One beer company made red bottles for a time in the 1950's and early 60's. It was called "Royal Ruby" bottles, made by Anchor Hocking.

In most cultures red is considered a strong color. It's come to denote the color of passion and love, or seduction; also violence, danger, anger, and adventure. Nine out of ten people when asked what first comes to mind in an open question, "Red is the color of what?"

Their answer is, "Blood."

THROUGH NEW GLASS CLEARLY

By the time 2016 is reached the kids are scattering to different parts. Sherry becomes known as Miss Sherry, teaching four-year-olds in a pre-school.

In the foretold restoration of the Messiah's kingdom, the prophet Isaiah describes in chapter 11 one short portion of a verse reading, "*...and a little child shall lead them.*" And Jesus commands "*Let the little children come to me; do not hinder them, for the kingdom of God belongs to such as these.*" (Matthew 19:14)

The influence of little ones on adults is unexpected in this new venture. Sherry relearns lessons through the humble trust of these young ones. Children sent home with daily simple creations, songs learned, parables taught and Bible verses memorized reach parents. One example of the sway a four-year-old can have on adults comes through Grace. Grace is an only child who has an atypical fascination with this Jesus she learns of in story lessons in the gospels. Toward the end of a school year, during an Easter brunch with parents and kids, Grace's mom says, "Miss Sherry, I just have to tell you that Grace's excitement about all she's learned in class has spilled over into our house."

"Oh that's so good to hear."

"But I mean you have to know what it has done in our family."

"How's that?"

"Grace's excitement carries over through the weekends."

"Wow."

"And now the year is ending, we see we need to continue the Bible for Grace, because of her enthusiasm."

"She is the life of the class—especially Bible time. I've only seen this with kids a few times."

"Well this is what's going on. So we began to take her to Sunday School. What's interesting is, neither of us—my husband or I—had any Church in our lives growing up—neither one of us ever entered a church, except funerals and weddings. Well, while Grace went to Sunday School—we decided to take her locally every Sunday—after a few weeks of waiting in the car outside until she was done—we decided we would attend service inside during that hour. It took some time—about a month I guess—before both of us made a decision to follow Jesus."

Sherry stood stunned. "You're kidding."

"Not at all. It was like we were hanging around beside a creek—listening, understanding—and then we just fell in. That's the best way I can describe it. It was like the whole thing was planned—and now we see He planned it all. All three of us—our lives changed tremendously. Everything."

Three changed people are the result of the simplest input of Gospel lessons and Bible verses passed from a teacher, to a child, to her parents in the course of a pre-school year.

***

SIXTY
When we turned thirty
We spun that song long and often. Then that tune just
Stopped short
As the turntable resumed its turning
with the turn of the clock.
Today you sing "Sixty."
We recall you—on the inside sending us out—
Lunch held in hands, prayers of protection
And blessing—sending us out

To a world of broken boundaries, ruthless builders.
We recall you— on the outside pushing us in, too—
To dinner on the table, prayers of thanksgiving,
And blessing—pushing us in
From that world of broken boundaries, ruthless builders.
You spoke with the poetry of your life, still speak
Of the sometimes when it doesn't seem He answers,
reciting—"He is"—on the outside pushing us in,
On the inside sending us out.
You speak to us with poetry—
all you know of His unbroken devotion.

WHISPERS FROM ORWELL

She stands beside the kitchen stove in shorts and bare feet cooking by the sound of crackling oil in a pan, blonde hair with streaks of gray to her shoulders masking half of her profile. He sits scrolling through his phone. "Everyone's looking the other way. Burning, looting. Someone's got to stop this. People talking a lot, but don't seem to do anything."

"I don't get it."

"These mayors and governors won't let the president send the National Guard."

"You pay too much attention to the news. Give it a rest."

"I know. I'm a news junkie."

"You are. Why don't ya stop awhile. It's too much."

"Maybe." A minute passes. His eyes keep watch, thumb riffling. "These people in the restaurant business can't survive."

"A lot of people."

"It's over the top. Watch. Once the election's over, everything's going to change."

"Things 'll get better." A spoon drops to the oak floor by the stove. The dog moves toward it, sniffing. She bends, lifts, places it into the sink, opens a drawer and pulls out another. "Kodi I already fed you. You can't be hungry."

"Joe Biden sits in his basement. Belongs in a nursing home. He's the best they can put up? Three hundred thirty million people? Lifetime politicians—the worst. This guy's accomplished nothing."

Sherry breathes heavily.

"Listen to this. Quotes from George Orwell." He adjusts his voice tone, "*1984*: 'Who controls the past controls the future.'"

"What's that mean? I always hear that."

"Well people are trying to rewrite history, or conceal it.

These rioters are kids. They haven't learned anything in these schools. They're taught a lot of lies."

"Hmmm"

"Here's another." He looks at his wife. "Listening?"

"I'm listening."

"'There was truth and there was untruth, and if you clung to the truth even against the whole world, you were not mad.'"

"I remember reading that book—except it's the wrong year."

The sound of a mower down the street controls the back—round. It suddenly stops, and both of their awareness take notice as the songs of a few birds replace the droning.

"How about this one—'the very existence of external reality was tacitly denied by their philosophy. The heresy of heresies was common sense.'"

"Wait, Say that again."

Slower, clearer, he reads, "'The very existence of external reality was tacitly denied by their philosophy. The heresy of heresies was common sense.'"

"Boy that's true." She walks toward the table.

"Defunding police makes no sense. The world's gone crazy."

"A lot of craziness. Common nonsense."

"Lord come!" She moves back to the stove.

They sit again at that long kitchen table which for years was filled with growing chattering children. It's a Friday evening. Her back's against those French doors as shadowy mauve dusk looms with its hesitant pause—that enduring summer suspension that seems to hold the world in secure hands, that suspension between day and night, where outside scraps of surviving sun are smothered—nearly—by the shade of awnings of trees on the lawn. The music of a fusion of birds warbles on.

Open screens of mid-July inhale with soft wafts of humid, grass scented air. Wide fans spin above lit bulbs flickering the ceiling.

They sit again before their plates—fish, rice, greens. It's 2020.

Heads bow.

"You praying tonight?" he says, closing his phone, placing it aside.

She bows her head. "Father in Jesus' name thank you for this food. Let it be good for us. You always provide for us and we thank you for that. Please be near our loved ones wherever they are tonight, and speak to them Lord. Amen."

"Amen."

BRIEF FLIGHT

Some endure stormy flights,
lugging baggage, cramped;
bagging losses, tired.
From bumpy cloud banks
the pretty city's unseen,
and we've no guarantees
of journeys thunder-free
Soaring time to arrivals.
If we trust the pilot, we rest—
Hearing His voice promising
sure crossing, safe landing—
the home we've never seen.

EPILOGUE

CENTER MORICHES
Goodbye.
Watch for our ghosts in our town, Center Moriches,
Walking the walks we walked for forty years.
Watch as they pass,
Brush by whispers of the past
Along the wetlands! paths curving the turns of Terrel River.
Hear our voices, ghost whispers in the village.
Listen! our long laughs linger, echoing low-
A muted rumble, dull purring
outboard pushing us across Moriches Bay,
Down Orchard Neck Creek.
See us in the shoe prints of our years,
faces in joy's noisy pain
Playing with our children
Who've grown and since departed.
We've moved away, yet wanted to stay,
Left these streets, these fields we've loved,
Carrying pieces to greener ground,
Leaving those ghosts, those voices, those whispers
Of ourselves in our town, Center Moriches,
Goodbye.

***

A clear October sky—noon, blue. She walks the shore of her favorite Rhode Island beach, seven miles from home—Napatree Point, adjacent to Watch Hill, all the way to the point, and back. She's with her husband. She's found a few pieces of glass. Old fifteen year old Kodi can't walk these distances anymore with them. They climb the rise of the high dune, returning to Watch Hill, and stop, leaning on the split rail fence to look at the vista onto Block Island Sound, farther—the Atlantic, and then opposite onto Little Narragansett Bay.

"So clear. Can see Block Island."

"I can't."

Silence.

"Thought you might today."

"Nope."

Silence.

"How about Fishers Island?" He's pointing.

"Vague."

"Really?"

"It's like just a bluish-green slash."

"You can see the lighthouse- over here—Watch Hill Point?"

She turns, squints, focusing behind her sunglasses. She shakes her head, tightens her lips. "I see the land—only."

They turn and look Northwest across Little Narragansett Bay. He stretches his arm moving his face close to hers, pointing. "Can you see that whitish spot there, where we launch the boat- at Barn Island?"

Focusing, searching—"All I see is all he green of Barn Island."

He shifts. "You see all the white buildings there? Stonington Borough?"

"Yeah I see that. A little blurry."

"How about Sandy Point Island—here—that white-green line—closer?

"A little."

He looks toward the closer village of Watch Hill. She follows. Can you see the big yellow hotel—up there?" He's pointing again.

She looks.

"The highest spot—there!"

"Yeah I think so."

"The flag blowing around on top?"

"No—no way—not at all."

Since her fourth decade of life this twenty five year contest with Sherry's pigmentary glaucoma has her backed into the corner of the fighting arena. As time has passed the elevated eye pressure has threatened damage to the optic nerves of both eyes, and treatment has grown aggressive. In time, tens of thousands of eye drops have fallen from her varied prescription bottles. Laser and incisional surgery, including glaucoma stents, drainage implants have been incisionally inserted. Sherry is so appreciative, filled with marvel of her eye doctors who study eyes, who look, themselves seeing carefully into the intricacies of her eyes, remedying afflictions there. She's always kept in mind the enduring statistic that glaucoma remains the leading cause of blindness.

She's endured five surgeries into her eyes, that main aim being to keep pressure in the eyes down, keeping away damage to the optic nerves. Sherry's peripheral vision has had significant increase in narrowing. She regularly visits an ophthalmologist in Westerly and a glaucoma specialist/surgeon in Providence. This eye disease, besides the peripheral narrowing, causes symptoms of extreme near blinding brightness because of the way light disperses on the eyes. This coerces her to wear prescribed sunglasses with special polarized lenses often, even in fluorescent lighted indoors.

Because of photosensitivity to glare, Sherry the patient has trouble with daily activity—a disability driving, an inability to drive at night. Glare causes intense discomfort. Seeing in semidarkness is impossible. She often moves in total blindness in dim light, feeling her way slowly.

Sharpness in visionary things- in depths, shapes, colors of objects and print gradually dulls. Without very large print on computer screens and paper, Cliff reads aloud to her. Her losses have grown more noticeable. She's aware. It has all regressed gradually.

A breeze exhales feebly from the bay side, softly lifts her hair, his, grasses on the dune. There's that sweet, briny, brackish smell. She says, "For some reason God is allowing this. I never thought He'd be refusing me the pleasure of the view."

"I'm sorry."

They're silent.

"Love the smell in the air," he says. "It must be like a prison for you."

"Not really. Not at all that way—yet anyway. Just a little confining now. Just hope it doesn't all close in entirely before the end."

He reaches around her shoulder, pulling her close, kisses the side of her head. She tilts it onto his shoulder.

2021. The grown "kids" have flown away, and Sherry and Cliff move away, retiring across the Long Island Sound to rural coastal Connecticut, on the Rhode Island border. The world's crazed upside down turn incited them to sell the house in Center Moriches. The house in Prince Edward Island is sealed up as the border is closed until the "pandemic" ends.

The road rolls east to west through Stonington township which distends beside the Pawcatuck River—dividing Connecticut from Rhode Island—flowing into the Atlantic, rolls along a hilly road painted in gray stony greenness in southeast Connecticut—a tiny dash found upon the vast reaches of this small planet in our solar system, a brief blink—infinitesimal—against the greater vastness expanding the cosmos. Predestined for the two of them and their fifteen year old dog, their new home—stowed in a secluded four acre forest by Little Narragansett Bay—is agreeably quiet.

Winter

Four acres. Stone. Woods—evergreens, oaks, swamp maples, wild cherry, bitter sweet, poison ivy, and cat brier descend a far slow slope toward the Amtrak curving through the base of a deep ravine. Trains race snowfall this day, this first winter, snow piling high an afternoon of forlorn forecasts. She listens within closed windows, planted in their new dwelling; hears one in the distance from their rooms of quiet—the Boston to New London run, speeding down beyond the steep end of their wooded acreage. Its velocity into distance separates swiftly as she feels its motion, smooth faint rumble, distant rhythmic rush.

The train—a new sound—races snowfall this afternoon.

Sun flurries, where flashes of sun send light into falling white, burst through clouds with brilliance, break open charcoal darkness of snow clouds, which somehow send this purity in weighty whiteness this afternoon. The sharp swift train passes with speed, cutting through winter like slices of knives through white fish.

She's not alone—her husband beside, fingers woven together. Of course this tonnage, this mechanism of power heard from a distance from above, their house on the hill and through the woods, the third that passes this day, speeds with a rush, muffled by woods, upon her hearing—in an all of a suddenness—a quiet surprise, like a gust of wind that sneaks upon you brazenly. Through new glass, snow-whiteness outside windows widens her indoor world, this express train—a surprise reminding of stations to come by, final destinations, longed for places where faces await her arrival at the end of the long railroad line of life.

Spring

Nothing ever changes. Nothing changes, ever. Never does anything change. Blue Jays scream this morning.

Most humans are sleeping. Blue birds feed in the cherry blossoms. The early morning's blue sun's hands hold her, and the flow of cold water falls into soil from the water can held in her hand.

Like a child holding cotton candy—she carries lavender lilac blossoms upright. Water showers, mist leaps, Light frames a tiny rainbow. It's an early May morning.

So it's a new state, town, a new home, a lot of newness; yet these changes have a way of reminding her that nothing ever changes, that their lives remain stable, still eternal. Behind her in high tall limbs lofty air blows and moves swiftly as angels, flinging fragrance, tossing subtle blossoms. Stiff, sinuous, tapered limbs lean forward.

Pushes, brushes of breezes from the sea press against trees, and her; greenness lilts; new buds of evergreens open in yellow. He watches her, his wife, her ardent movement as she shines through lucid breakfast glass in green honesty, in the expanse of their greening yard. Hair lifts behind her, shining aglow against white cotton—contrast like those petals of cherry blossoms against the pastel expanse of sky, against flutters of florescent blue bird wings.

Hours will pass; noon will come; night will fall; summer will come; seasons will pass. Life will continue to intrude with its ritual revolution, its flurries of spores, organisms, sore hearts and old scores, but she knows—nothing important ever changes. God's stability reigns.

Summer

Ripe wild blackberries. She gently holds each between fingers, pulls, and each falls with scarcely a resistant cling into her palm. Filling a bowl in open sun, it seems the unready reds ripen unbidden, blackening before her eyes, as she leans fumbling in simmering heat through brambles, unhurried.

They drop some onto their tongues, talking of former years—old blackberry patches left somewhere almost lost in their memory, like fallen berries left to seed the spongy mulch beneath. Reaching deeper canes from this path she doesn't dare tug them close as thorny tangles prick skin.

She stretches, leaning at length—inside, careful, lower, searching beneath scribbles of shadows under canes, glowering with her green eyes glancing upward, kneeling to rest in this crisscross of brake in shade, gazing farther through overhead canopies of trees, through a hundred shades of green, into sure steady blue.

It's the heat that seems to slow the pace. Shorter walks reduced to strolls, a ride on the boat, air conditioning, meals in restaurants, trips to the doctors. The big concern is the growing pressure in her eyes demanding drops, pills, surgical procedures, aims at halting the ever present progression of glaucoma. There's always something that she has learned keeps her closely dependent on her God.

Autumn

The truth is that somehow sometime something went terribly wrong in all of our lives somewhere, since the beginning—the very beginning. It was disclosed in coal—black inside all of us, wrenching us humans far apart, from each other, from our creator. We've tried to define its wily primitiveness with vivid words in philosophic explanations. Someone great and heroic came to reprise us in our own tragedy, binding those of us who are inclined—as friends to the end.

They walk across a field on the nearby Barn Island, a twelve hundred acre Connecticut preserve. On a far perimeter blazing yellow trees gleam. Shadows of sugar maples that had shaded them in cool, sky-blue rest on a simmering summer afternoon months earlier, are now softened. Fall's gold calls them where underneath they wonder how sun paints a lucid hue, actually changing them. Their skin seems strangely tinted—a faint, dull, yellow glow.

But she's aging. He's aging. They know it, without balking at it. They at all times hoped to grow old together. Here they are as their mingled plot has thickened, as each gray hair's a new event, each wrinkle a page, each scar a chapter pacing at fever pitch toward their lives' stories' resolutions where theme comes clear, and their book will close.

Time, it seems, is a swift river that drifts westward, a steady stream whose watery hours never reverse, always in a kind of November—with its noticeable gradual lessening light, in gradual lengthening night, day following night following day. On favored days, good and pleasant daylight hours, we wish this stream could freeze thoroughly through down to its bottom. To freeze time, to keep those moments, those days, years—as maybe a photo seizes those passing moments that float by in life—to hold forever. That would find favor, we suppose.

On weary days, on bad and unpleasant days we wish the earth could tilt, and the river tip and flow backward, behind—to an earlier time, back to fairer pastures, to passages of the past. As Robert Frost says, "It's when we're weary of considerations, and life is too much like a pathless wood."

One someday a dawn will rise into a beautiful clearing, and this stream of time will spill into a crystal sea; We'll wear new clothes, on new physical frames. We'll bear new names. What's good, true, and right will all be new and permanent, *"and there will be no night there."*

***

2024—And where did all the "kids" fly?

Sarah who married Matt are in Maine, both teaching, splitting wood, loading the stove, dressing warm, and raising two girls—Mercy and Clare. Their adopted, Kalaeb, has grown and moved to Texas.

Laura, married to John, is in California, a social worker and therapist—raising little Emma, a smart little princess.

Thomas is a teacher who's remained on Long Island, is often out bowling, or gone fishing, or spending time with his little dog, Peanut.

Zachary too is still near the old house on Long Island. He's the artist—art teacher who's traveled from Iceland to Japan to in-between.

Abby the RN who married Steven the graphic designer—moved to our neighborhood, with Finn who's nearly a year old—the jolliest little chap in Connecticut, making us the happiest—finally having a Grandchild nearby—only three miles away.

Gabriel is in Maryland—a Navy veteran, and now a technician repairing hospital laboratory equipment.

Samuel the soccer star is now on the flight deck of the *George H. Bush* carrier, sometimes in Norfolk, Virginia; sometimes somewhere in the Mediterranean Sea.

All seven come to visit their old parents here in Connecticut. Sometimes they all visit at the same time.

And of course our second-born Rebekah, for forty years now, remains safe in that place with "Jesus… the bright and Morning Star" where "*They shall see His face, and His name shall be on their foreheads. And there shall be no night there…*" (Revelation 22:4,5). It's that place we call home, the home we haven't yet seen, but are strangely homesick for.

AFTERWARD

Added by Sherry Schrage specifically for her children and grandchildren—a mom's heart and a grammy's joy

SARAH ELIZABETH

Our first gift—the joy of finding out I was carrying you was overwhelming, not something I was eager to be done with. Feeling all your movements inside was a delight. You stayed there two weeks beyond your due date. I worked full time just before the day came when regular contractions began. I was scared. 36 hours of labor until a C-section was needed. Waking, a nurse said, "You have a baby boy." I thought, no way. I was convinced you were a girl. Later, "Sorry, it's a girl, 9 pounds, 12 oz," she said. You were the biggest in the nursery. How funny, now a petite woman. I loved holding you, staring at your beautiful face those days, healing. Being 24, nervous and excited, I had questions—how was I going to be a mother? I wanted to protect you. Bringing you home was scary, but we figured it out.

You grew, and it became obvious that you were smart—talking, singing song lyrics when you were only one. You grew to love books, play imaginatively alone. We walked trails, the beach—intrigued with nature.

But first, at 16 months your life changed quite a bit

when your sister Rebekah was born. All those months I was sick in the hospital—and in the hospital with her—stressful for us all, maybe mostly for you. Dad always put the phone to your ear to talk to me. Separated, when you saw things that reminded you of me—a coat, shoes... you would cry. You spent a lot of time with Dad. Family cared for you many weeks on and off while Dad was with me and your sister in Stony Brook.

It was a wonderful day when I could finally be with you, holding you at home. When Rebekah came you had another adjustment as she needed care. You wanted to help—as a one-year-old once slipping a can of cat food into her crib. That spring we walked Rebekah a lot and played in the yard. But life became more difficult when she was hospitalized for months, and then passed away. You became my reason to get out of bed. I loved you, knowing you needed me more than ever. I tried to give you focused attention, even while my heart was broken.

Letting you go, sending you to school was made easier when I saw you loved it—art, reading, flute, making friends—roller skating, soccer, especially in high school— mission trips to Guatemala and Ireland—with people you didn't know—very brave, canoeing across the bay, a lot of laughter with your friends.

The first to leave the nest, off to college in Massachu-setts, I cried the whole drive home. I loved to hear your voice when you called and spoke of good friends you made, and have kept. Your attending Oxford for a year was exciting for me as it was for you, along with all your travel there. I loved those sent postcards, your own paintings. You had concern for people, were kind to your siblings as they entered our family. You were a big supporter of our adoptions, even though it meant sharing a room, helping more, and maybe foregoing attention for yourself.

Flashbacks of you riding the rear seat on my bike through Center Moriches, reading books to you with your head against me, hearing the made-up songs you sang alone: "It's raining. It's dark out. I love you," the entertaining shows you put on in the yard, your green clip-on earrings, your desire for "diamond teeth" (braces), praying with you at bedtime… are just some that will never go away from my memory.

You held my hand during part of your wedding ceremony. I was happy you and Matt found each other. I love talking to you about the many subjects that you are interested in. You have many carefully thought-out ideas and information on many interesting topics. You haven't had it easy, becoming deathly ill from Lymes, and more—doing all the research while you were sick, when doctors there in Maine weren't much help, all the effects on family life, and your work as a teacher. Sarah: "God's Princess," makes you special. "The Lord with arise upon you, and His glory will be seen on you." (Isaiah 60:2)

LAURA GRACE

I remember our first adoption—when we were matched by the agency with you. I cried tears of joy receiving your photo in your infancy, having prayed that God would bring us the child He wanted for our home before I even knew who you were,. Anticipation was overwhelming, and I was naturally nervous about your being happy with us.

The night before receiving you at the airport had me concerned about my love for you the moment I held you. Silly. The moment I saw your little doll face I was filled with love, and still am. You had a rough adjustment. I held you as often as I could—even slept beside you on the mattress on the floor, as I'd learned how families slept together in South Korea.

You hated the car when you were a baby. I often reached my hand to pat your leg so you wouldn't be afraid. As a toddler, saying "Bopweeze" you often pushed past everyone to get to the car first. All through elementary school you disliked dresses and frilly things. You loved the swings—swinging as high as you could. We always had a stack of library books in your room—never enough to read for you. A good student, friend, and helper in school, you were always bringing friends to youth group. I think your detective birthday party was your favorite—having a lot of fun preparing for it. Your fear of clowns at age three brought you to bite Dad's leg once on Halloween when you both answered the door finding a big clown there looking at you. You loved fishing with Dad, once catching a duck. What a mess, and you fell into the water off your chair. You were only three. Your surprise 17th birthday, "Super seventeen" really was a true surprise as you saw all your friends. It was a well-kept secret.

You grew to become especially beautiful in appearance, very smart, athletic, and competitively hard working—striving to be first in everything you did—on the soccer field, reading competitions, academic grades. I remember your love of singing—fond of hearing your voice as you were arriving from school walking down the driveway, singing—always, in the house, yard, car…

We were so proud at your graduation—Salutatorian 2005—Center Moriches HS, accepted into the US Coast Guard Academy—leaving us the day following graduation that June. I realized that day in the kitchen that I wouldn't hear your singing anymore, and remember the tears as we left you at the academy in New London, unable to communicate for forthcoming months because of the rigors you were facing. We all made it through that time.

God has taken you on journeys for sure, and we went through some rough waters. I always prayed for you, that you would remain close to Jesus. Becoming a supervising social worker, and beginning a counseling practice has been challenging for you; and your walking through many fiery trials has made you stronger, wiser, and dependent on God. Amazed by your faith and strength (physically fit strength too) Laura, "Victory," has proven valid. You encourage me, always caring; I love the regular phone calls as you drive from work, and we cherish our visits to San Diego. Your deep love for Emma is shown in the excellent care you give her. And your kind and gentle husband John has been a perfect ingredient into our family. Your name: Laura (from Laurel) "victorious" so aligns with your verse: "But thanks be to God who giveth us the victory through our Lord Jesus Christ." (1 Corinthians 15:57)

THOMAS NATHAN

From the start of your adoption until your arrival from South Korea took only nine months—the fastest process we've walked through. You were the easiest as a little one to care for—a very content and happy baby. You stayed awake through your first night. I reclined next to you on a quilt on the carpet thinking you'd eventually sleep. You didn't, but every night following you slept easily.

You were a happy child. At three you were a cowboy, wearing a hat, bandanna, denim, holster—the works—riding on a stick horse. Baseball was your passion in grade school. I'd pitch to you in the yard for hours while Dad was at work, winding up with a frozen shoulder, needing cortisone shots—ouch. It was worth it to see your joy. You really excelled in all you put your mind to—guitar, flute, drums, piano, skate boarding, magic tricks, rubrics cube—and your bowling a 299 and one perfect 300 score still amazes me. You were always doing—busy—and I can see how you bring all your joy with all these interests to your young students in your classroom.

I recall the first year in high school, and all four following—you were elected President of your class at Center Moriches HS, and we loved being in the audience as you performed in lead roles in the school plays and musicals. You were always very likable Tom. You were a gifted soccer player, part of one Long Island championship team; and you so loved baseball and basketball.

On your fifth birthday we woke up to a lot of snow, and you were so happy. I set the birthday table cloth and you said, "The snow is a present from God for me." A neighbor brought a coloring book and crayons, and you were so thrilled. Every little thing during that day I remember made you happy. We made a cake together and when your sisters and dad came home you said, "This is the best day."

You used to follow Dad around as he split wood, and you helped by dragging and stacking logs. You loved fishing and skating at Kaler's Pond, playing hockey for hours in cold weather—as soon as the pond froze—recruiting your brothers and friends. Once, without our knowing, out on the front lawn we heard a loud explosion. You said, "I was just making a chlorine bomb," like it was perfectly normal. When Zachary was a baby you sang to him—songs you made up like, "Zachary Zachary you are the cutest baby in the world." You were very protective over him when he was little.

Most important and worth noting, you were (and remain) very kind, often looking out for the kids who were lonely or outcast, befriending them—even in the deli you worked at through college years. We noticed that, and so does God. It was conspicuous to many that you were exceptionally gifted. I always cherish time we get to talk about books, your students, music, God… My happy sweet boy is a young man. Recent years have been bumpy—as life gets sometimes for you, but God is near. Your name: "Seeker of truth," is one I pray you will remain, fitting with your verse: "I shall seek You earnestly, to see Your power and glory." (Psalm 63:1,2)

ZACHARY JAMES

Your adoption took a long time. We prayed daily that you'd arrive soon. That sunny day finally came in God's timing. You were nine months old. We drove from the airport on the Robert Moses Causeway beside Zach's Bay. You were quietly observant, trying to understand who we were, where you were, what was happening. There were many things to get used to—smells, faces, foods. You were very loved, and you loved to be held and shown things in the house. I named everything you saw. At that age you could already pull yourself up to standing, holding onto furniture, walking.

You grew and loved to play, lining up cars so carefully, building blocks high, and looking through books. Growing older you loved the outdoors—the trees, fascination with bugs and creatures, and even the phases of the moon in the night sky. You somehow figured out how to pull webbing out of spiders, wrapping it around your finger. You collected bees, removing their stingers, collected crickets and butterflies. You often got me bouquets of flowers from the yard. I have a nice memory of driving to the sod farm with you and Tom in your teens, watching a meteor shower. We've taken a lot of walks together through the years. Of course, going to Iceland with your siblings and niece, watching the Northern lights is unforgettable.

As soon as you could hold a crayon drawing became your favorite. Once eating mashed potatoes you drew with your knife, saying, "Look I etched a pancreas." Funny. At age five your drawings became detailed—skyscrapers, ships, landscapes.... It wasn't hard to see you were artistic. You had quite an eye, once pointing at a crescent moon, "God's fingernail."

Donating shoes for children in an orphanage one year, we asked all the kids to donate some money, you went and got all your money, $120.00. You insisted you wanted to give all you had, understanding their need. Loving the beach, once in Maine you befriended a little girl, playing by the water whispering in each other's ears giggling all day.

You love fish, still love fishing with Dad, and you remain the one with the best fishing luck. You took good care of your fish tank. We had your "fish" birthday party, decorating the windows with fish in transparent paper, creating a cake with an underwater scene.

You were a serious thinker, once saying as an older child, "The deeper you look into human life you see it's nasty," trying to make sense of good and evil.

Your art brings happiness to people, like the mural you did for the school I worked at, and many other pieces you give and sell. I enjoy our talks about life, God, and art; and I appreciate many things more since seeing them through your artistic eyes. Also, your love of food and cooking blesses us.

God has a plan to continue growing His use of your talent for His purposes, as your name "Whom God remembers," states. Your scripture, "I have formed you. You are my servant. You will not be forgotten by Me." (Isaiah 44:21)

ABIGAIL FAITH

Description of how many things God put in place to bring you to our family is a long story. Right before we got a phone call about you, we had a placement of a little baby who ended up leaving us in a few weeks to be placed with his family member. My heart broken, I said, "I can't do this again." Coming home late from a trip a social worker called saying there was a baby girl who needed a home. After a few questions, we decided we should. You arrived the next day—our first foster-to-adopt (not foreign), two weeks old with dark thick hair and a pretty face, and we had an immediate bond. Only God knew the battle we were to face in the early process of adopting you.

Not long after, we were engaged in stressful birth-parent visits—for three years, with court hearings and agency meetings. (You know some details) But the day the judge finally decided to terminate birth parent rights and free you for adoption came as a sudden surprise and a relief, welcomed at our door by the social worker who felt it worth the trip from New York City to bring the news. Years of late-night prayer and fears of your being removed from us were over. Uncle Gary brought over a cake that night with your name on it. When adoption was settled at age 6, the time of Gabe's adoption too, a huge celebration followed with 150 friends and family, a whole day filled with memorable fun for kids: ponies, cotton candy, popcorn, Elmo, Easter egg hunting, and much more.

Your dressing up for tea parties, forcing Gabe to attend, are memories that stay with me. Our mission trips together to Central America are clear. I loved that my help to plan your wedding was something you welcomed—seeing you in the dress you chose, how radiant you looked, and how thankful you were that we could get it. Your happiness on your big day—dancing with your siblings, Emma looked at you in awe. You looked "like a princess." In Canada, you loved beach walks, biking, and of course, running. You always looked out for Sam. Once at three, you said, "One of my wishes is that the sky is low so we could touch it. That's why a giant could pick us up and we could touch it, and touch God."

You chanted your phonics charts in the car: "_Sh_ in ship. _Tr_ in truck…" Over and over. Gabe, wearied, shouted, "_Uff_ in enough!" On a field trip your rock candy dripped down your neck. You cried, "Can I die from a sticky neck?" At seven you began asking advanced questions, like "Why would God create the world if He knew we would sin?"

Your years at school clearly showed how smart God made you—passing over second grade because of lack of challenge; then doubling up, bypassing a year in high school—graduating two years early, finishing early from college, and accelerated nursing, making you an RN in less than five years, at 21, entering hospital nursing when COVID began. I'm so proud. Your gift at giving—in care taken for fitting gifts and words to bless people—doesn't go unnoticed.

Marrying Stephen, a wonderful husband, buying a home near us in Connecticut, bringing our grandson Finn into our world has made me the happiest—finally having a grandchild nearby. While life brings storms and challenges, I pray you grow into looking to God for strength.

Your name: "Her father's joy," has proven true in too many ways. Your verse: "No weapon formed against you shall prosper." (Isaiah 54:17) continues to prove true.

GABRIEL JOSEPH

You were the tiniest infant, Gabe. Your little life didn't begin with ease, as you needed much care from the start. Your older siblings always talked to you in those earliest days. It's hard to believe you're now 6'4"

We all recall your love of cars—your earliest ability to identify makes and models. You had an unusual knack at remembering road directions even on long trips—this innate awareness of geography.

I have fond memories. Once when you were three you put your small brown hand by mine, saying, "We're the same color." I won't forget your spending earned lemonade money at a garage sale down the road in Canada to buy me a pretty green bowl. You wanted me on all your field trips. Coming out of the pool at dusk once when you were four you said, "The sun is dead." At eight you gave yourself a haircut. I was horrified. You thought it would be good to go in the bathroom and smear toothpaste on your head. Without telling me you once gave your favorite Matchbox Ferrari for the orphan's shoebox. You did some nice things, fun and funny things. Once driving home from Canada at a rest area, Dad had a sentimental moment, saying that he loved you and would do anything for you all, you responded to Dad, "Will you buy us ice cream, Dad?"

You often loved dressing up for school—wearing a tie and jacket—when you were very young, and continued with fashion. As a child, through your teens, into early adulthood, your love of reading brought you into getting happily lost in books—for hours, unable to stop until books were finished—under late-night flashlights at times. Another actor and singer in the high school productions, we'll never forget your senior year lead as Horton, singing with a powerful strong voice.

You had an unusual healthy quest to try new sports each season, to give a try at as many different sports as you could through high school: volleyball, football, basketball, lacrosse, soccer, baseball, track, changing year by year with an adventurous spirit.

Deciding in high school you wanted to start in the military (Navy), we said goodbye and waited weeks to hear from you, until your phone call said you worked through boot camp successfully. Witnessing your ceremony in Chicago filled us with pride and happiness for you. You accomplished what you aimed for, then endured the longest record deployment at sea—without going to port—extremely difficult for all on that ship during COVID. It was a great day when you returned.

The Navy behind you now, having the obstacle of being diagnosed with diabetes—you persevere, and work now servicing medical equipment, with the uncertainty of its being your life's career. God knows what's ahead. As long as you look to Him, he will help you through. Your name and verse: "God is my strength," is so apt for your verse, "for you have given me strength for the battle." (2 Samuel 22:40)

SAMUEL ELSHADAY

Seeing your picture Sam, our youngest, with your stuffed animal, and learning of your story—coming to the United States once, but not finding a family in a matching program is what made us move toward you after praying. Meeting you when you were five in Ethiopia, you seemed shy. You had us fooled. By the time we brought you to the hotel in Addis Ababa, you were a package of energetic noise, tearing into everything, wild, almost impossible to control, jumping on beds, always running.

Finally getting you home that June, after ten days we were exhausted, and you were just starting—so much newness for you. We all remember those first several days—your astonishment at our plenty. You used to repeatedly open the refrigerator doors, and just look, eyes absorbing the vision of food. You explored cabinets, closets. You were amazed we had two cars, and a dog—imagine—inside the house. You fell in love with Slurpees, requesting two at 7-11. The language was difficult for you, but eventually we could communicate. You told us of weather in Ethiopia: "Rain. No snow. Rain. Yeah, hundred times rain! The rain is God peeing." We bonded during that summer at the Prince Edward Island house, as you learned some language skills before school was to begin, learned how to ride your bike, fish, dig clams, steer the boat, ride the tube, swim. You loved returning to that place each summer following. Our long morning walks on the beach—just the two of us—were very special to me, especially your expressing details of the difficult beginning you remembered in Ethiopia. I'm happy you felt safe to tell me. And I loved listening as you spoke of the things you hoped for for your future.

You had a reckless prowess with athletic ability. We were all very impressed with your doing forward flips on the beach, landing on your feet with unruffled finesse. But it did seem like we spent a lot of time in emergency rooms, orthopedic offices, and oral surgeon's waiting rooms through your youth, repairing all your injuries.

Soccer was your love, as it was all you had at the orphanage; and you brought that love and skill to our Long Island. We remember you on the local teams literally dribbling the ball around the other players through the years. We'll never forget your scoring the only two winning goals in the Long Island championship game for Center Moriches—your final year. A lot of well-deserved press. A lot of injuries on the field too—like Tom and Gabe. You loved school because you loved being with other kids; but learning came difficult for you, as you tried very hard.

You're all grown up, serving in the Navy. Your willingness to serve, perhaps encouraged by your brother Gabe, really makes us proud. Your special personality and love for laughing is contagious. You are very loved, Sam. Your name:

"God has heard," is proven as He has heard your cries in your earliest youth, giving you a hope and a future. "God has heard," is what I pray you'll always remember, reminding you that He always hears. Your verse: "May the God of peace sanctify you completely; He who calls you is faithful, who also will do it" (1 Thessalonians 5:23-24) is a promise.

KALEAB DAVID

Our oldest grandchild, your story here began when we went to bring our Sam home from Ethiopia. We met you, age ten then, in the orphanage the day we brought toys to the kids. One gift was bottles of bubbles, and we were one short, leaving one younger child in tears. You stepped in, Kaleab, handing over yours willingly. We were amazed at how self-lessly you assisted with the smaller ones; at a time, you may have understood you had begun to come to the age of being less adoptable. We spoke no Amharic, but you spoke some English. You told us you loved soccer (turned out like Sam you too were exceptional, winning Maine State awards); you loved school, and wished to someday be adopted.

When we left, wishing we could adopt you as well, we promised to look for a home for you. As you know, just mentioning it to our oldest Sarah, married three years, expecting their first baby, she and Matt came to us saying they felt like they were supposed to adopt you. Wow. The process began, and you came two years later, to a big, extended, close family. We were all so happy. Sam was very excited to see you again, and there was a lot of joking that you would be calling him Uncle Sam, being years older than him. (Mookie Cisek was very excited to see you too.) You've grown into a fine young man, attending college, then moving to Texas to work in the computer industry. We're proud of you, and happy you make travel time to visit us when you can.

MERCY ANNA

Not oldest, but first grandchild, to say I was "over the

moon with joy" when we heard you were coming puts it mildly. I walked around in a daze not totally believing. We began to pray for you then—daily—and haven't stopped since. You were the sweetest and cutest. You made us laugh a lot. I loved to hold you and never wanted to let you go. It has been one of my greatest joys watching you grow into a beautiful, kind, patient young woman. I have many memories of playing with you—the tea parties, games, the beach, the lake, making slime (our first failure thrown into the woods stayed colorful there a long time) Picking berries, and making muffins stand out as fun times. Your responsible care of all your ducks and your guinea pigs through the years is so noticeable. We love driving up to watch you play soccer and run track. Our mutual love of collecting sea glass is something that makes me happy. You have the best eye for them hidden in the stones at the beach. I'm so happy we got to visit Iceland together, seeing the Northern lights those nights. You have remained the same sweet girl, and my heart is so happy when I get to see you. Love you so much, and I look forward to seeing what God has planned for you.

CLARE JANE

Our second granddaughter is one we were so excited about when we knew you were to be born. Our "shy" Clare, born in Maine, far enough to make our visits rarer—made those times ones I just wanted to really be "in the moment." You so loved Kodi our dog, never afraid of him. You have a wonderful love for animals, like the little birds that fly into your open hand filled with seeds. I loved all your imaginary play, playing "dress up" and taking you to the store when you were younger—for that princess dress, and crown, and jewels. I remember you asked me if I thought you were beautiful, and I said, "You are beautiful." You still are beautiful dear Clare. Poppy must have played hide and seek with you 100 times, indoors and out. I am amazed at all the books you read, and your unique love of your pet dragon-lizard George and guinea pigs is so nice to watch. Your discovery of choir, and

playing a part in a play, singing solo—these have revealed
that you're really not shy, but quiet and thoughtful. You have
such a sense of humor making you fun to be with, and it
shows your happiness. I love you, and am so thankful to have
you as my granddaughter.

EMMA JOY

Emma Joy, our sweet, energetic, funny girl. When
Mommy told me she was expecting you she said she hadn't
told anyone yet and wanted to wait awhile. Well, I was so
excited and had to tell someone, so I told the checkout girl in
the supermarket, and other strangers I'd met because I
couldn't contain my joy. I couldn't wait to see you, making
plans to fly to San Diego to see you that weekend you were
born, but as you delivered early, I got to see you at five
days—a very content baby, eating, and sleeping. We've tried
to see you as often as possible, being 3000 miles away, but
are so grateful for FaceTime. We recall so much fun packed
into our visits—your many stuffed animals, play kitchen,
always serving meals on the little plates, trips to the zoo and
aquarium, your favorite songs like "Baby Shark" hearing
repeatedly, Poppy giving you rides across your big floor,
your bedtime stories and prayers. A smart little girl who loves
school, reading, singing, putting on shows, swimming and
gymnastics. Doing crafts, baking, and games are activities I
love with you. So happy you fly to visit us sometimes too,
and I look forward to more time with you. I love you, Emma
Joy.

FINN STEPHEN

How blessed are we to have you in our lives sweet
Finn—living only three miles away—and to take care of you
while Mommy works. I was fortunate to hold you, rock you,
and feed you the very first day you were born—the first for
me with grandchildren. Observing the daily changes in your
development has been heartwarming. Watching you observe

the world—wind in the trees, leaves falling, snowflakes blowing, birds flying... is wonderful. Your love of the stroller—never stopping—and the car—never red lights—keeps you smiling. Your bursts of hysterical laughter at silly unexplainable things is a fun mystery to us all. What's so funny? You love to chase your dog Riley now that you can crawl. I love to watch your expressions as you anticipate the next page while reading to you. Peek-a-boo makes me laugh with you as you are the jolliest little boy. My heart is full every day I spend with you. Now that Grammy's older, hopefully wiser, I take each day one at a time, enjoying you, knowing how quickly time goes. Holding you is more than I could ask for. God is so very good to allow me the privilege of caring for you. I look forward to each step forward with you, praying always for God's hand of protection over you. I love you little Finn.

ONE DAY

One night you're kissing his head, rocking him back to sleep, until time quietly passes into years, and he no longer needs your midnight rescue.

One day you're playing "This Little Piggy"; then you're buying her first school shoes. One moment you're playing blocks, then the next you are putting your backpack on for school. One evening you're singing in chorus, and then what seems suddenly, you're receiving your diploma.

One day you're holding his hand crossing the street; then quietly, abruptly, it seems he's off driving himself down the street. One Saturday they were playing dress up, and then another not-so-distant Saturday later, you watch them walk down an aisle, becoming someone's wife.

You're playing *Peek-a-Boo* with the ten-month-old, and soon after he's off down the street to play basketball with friends. She's spilling words of what's bothering her in the middle school, and next—you're leaving her off at college. He runs to you in diapers for a hug; and then it seems he's running onto a bus, not looking back.

Each day—it passes—and you barely notice change, until a milestone, and you wonder where those moments of days go. In your heart and mind, you know you tried never to forget the small moments, like the sweetness of their small hands reaching for you. As years and changes come it's hard to remember the accumulations of the *in-betweens*. You want to remember the hugs, words, laughs, and gestures… but they all blur into the day-to-day busy existence of survival. You wish every moment to be clenched, frozen—like that bouquet of dandelions carefully fisted, the smile, that laugh, the wet little frame shivering after a bath, wrapping her in a towel, holding her close as she lay her head on your shoulder. You want the bedtime stories and prayers, each little voice talking to God… all those moments, so fleeting. As Dad expresses, "Time flies. One winter afternoon you're in your 20's in the yard. Overhead geese cast loud shadows. You glance, squint. They fly away. Suddenly somehow, you're in your 60's."

One day the Lego creations displayed in rooms filled with treasures of rocks, cars, stick-guns, favorite stuffies—all gone. Tea parties carefully set on little tables, invitations scribbled in crayon, cookies, water poured by small hands, dolls in chairs—all vanished. One day the science fair projects and ribbons won for hard work—gone; packages wrapped hidden with instructions not to look under the bed; Christmas stockings, and the happiness for trinkets and candy—one day all walked away. One day the Easter egg coloring done uniquely by each artist washes away; loud dinner table conversations, all talking at once about the day's events—fade into silence. Many happy birthday celebrations; kindergarten through college graduations—seem gone in the twinkling of the eye.

One day you wake up and the house is empty; the hugs, tears, laughs, shouts have disappeared. With many emotions through forty years, I see you—all my children—loved so much that at times I felt my heart would break. Prayers for you continue, and now for your children too. Life is so fleeting, over which no one has control. I've learned to leave you in God's care, praying you always search for Him who truly loves you. I pray that in some way I have been used by Him in your lives, and have made a small dent into the fallen world by loving you.

www.ingramcontent.com/pod-product-compliance
Lightning Source LLC
Chambersburg PA
CBHW051158120626
46547CB00012B/1112